Constitutional Law in Portugal

Constitutional Law in Portugal

Third Edition

Jorge Bacelar Gouveia

This book was originally published as a monograph in the International Encyclopaedia of Laws/Constitutional Law.

Founding Editor: Roger Blanpain
General Editor: Frank Hendrickx
Volume Editors: André Alen & David Haljan

Wolters Kluwer

Published by:
Kluwer Law International B.V.
PO Box 316
2400 AH Alphen aan den Rijn
The Netherlands
E-mail: international-sales@wolterskluwer.com
Website: lrus.wolterskluwer.com

Sold and distributed in North, Central and South America by:
Wolters Kluwer Legal & Regulatory U.S.
7201 McKinney Circle
Frederick, MD 21704
United States of America
Email: customer.service@wolterskluwer.com

Sold and distributed in all other countries by:
Air Business Subscriptions
Rockwood House
Haywards Heath
West Sussex
RH16 3DH
United Kingdom
Email: international-customerservice@wolterskluwer.com

Printed on acid-free paper

ISBN 978-90-411-9616-3

e-Book: ISBN 978-90-411-9617-0
web-PDF: ISBN 978-90-411-9618-7

Printed in the United Kingdom.

The Author

Jorge Bacelar Gouveia (born 1 July 1966) studied law at the Faculty of Law of the University of Lisbon, Portugal, where he graduated in Law in 1989 and subsequently obtained a Masters in Public Law in 1993. He lectured there from 1989 to 1997.
He joined the Faculty of Law of the *Universidade Nova de Lisboa* (New University of Lisbon), Portugal when it was founded, and obtained, in 1999, a doctorate (PhD) in Public Law from that university, with a thesis in the field of Constitutional Law. He was immediately promoted to Full Professor of Law in this the most modern public teaching and research Faculty of Law in Portugal.
Since then, he has lectured in various public law subjects such as Constitutional Law, International Public Law, Administrative Law, Tax Law and Financial Law. He has published extensively (over 150 titles) both in Portugal and abroad. His main publications, with several editions, are *Manual de Direito Internacional Público* and *Manual de Direito Constitucional* (Handbook of Public International Law and Handbook of Constitutional Law).
He has collaborated with universities in Portuguese-speaking countries, namely in Brazil, Angola and Mozambique, where he has directed research projects and law specialization programmes, as well as lectured at legal seminars.
He is also chairman of the Portuguese Institute of Public Law, an association of public law specialists, which aims to promote and develop Public Law research in Portugal. He is the editor of *Revista de Direito Público*, the only Portuguese journal, at national level, with a particular focus on the various Public Law fields and related subjects.

The Author

Table of Contents

The Author 3

List of Abbreviations 11

Preface 13

General Introduction 15

§1. The Birth and Evolution of Portugal 15

§2. Portuguese Citizenship 17

§3. Portuguese Sovereignty 18

§4. The Portuguese Territory 20

§5. Shaping and Evolution of the Portuguese Constitution 21

§6. The Republican, Democratic and Semi-presidential Political System 24

§7. Unitarian Structure of the Portuguese State and Minor Political Entities 25

Part I. Sources of Portuguese Law 27

Chapter 1. The Constitution as the Main Source of Portuguese Constitutional Law 27

§1. General Meaning of Constitution 27

§2. The Constitution as Law of the State 28

§3. The Constitution as the Supreme Act of Public Law 29

§4. The Constitution as the Core of the Positive Legal Order 30

§5. The Constitution as Legal Code 31

Chapter 2. Constituent Power and Constitutional Reform 34

§1. Constituent Power and the Birth of the Constitution 34

§2. The Characteristic Features of Constituent Power 35

§3. Particular Manifestations of the Constituent Power 36

§4. Constitutional Reform 37

§5. Entrenched Matters and Constitutional Reform 39

§6. The Hyper-rigidity of the Portuguese Constitution 42

Chapter 3. The Secondary Sources of Portuguese Constitutional Law 43

§1. The Diminished Relevance of Constitutional Custom 43

§2. Practical Limitation of Constitutional Jurisprudence 45

§3. Exclusion of Other Sources of Constitutional Law 47

Chapter 4. The Non-constitutional Sources of Portuguese Law 50

§1. General Framework of the Public Law Functions and Acts and Their Hierarchy 50

§2. International Function and International Conventions 51

§3. Legislative Function and Legislative Acts 53

§4. Political Function and Political Acts 53

§5. Administrative Function and Administrative Acts 54

§6. Judicial Function and Judicial Acts 55

Chapter 5. Legislative Function, Legislative Acts and in Particular Legislative Procedure 56

§1. Definition of the Legislative Function 56

§2. Reserved Matters and Lawmaking Competence 57

§3. The Types of Legislative Acts 59

§4. The Organic Laws in Particular 61

§5. The Lawmaking Process 62

Part II. The Portuguese Political System 65

Chapter 1. The Portuguese Democracy 65

§1. Portugal as a Democratic State 65

§2. Representative Democracy and Elections 67

§3. The Fundamental Features Of Portuguese Electoral Law 69

§4. Semi-direct Democracy and the Referendum 72

§5. Fundamental Elements of the Portuguese Law on Referendums 73

§6. Participative Democracy and Political Parties 78

§7. The New Political Parties Law in Portugal 81

Chapter 2. Portuguese Organs of Government 87

§1. The President of the Republic 87

§2. Assembly of the Republic 90

§3. The Government 93

§4. Courts of Law 97

§5. The Constitutional Court 99

§6. Other Organs of Government 101

Part III. The Portuguese State and Its Internal Organization 105

Chapter 1. The Fundamental Options in the Form of the Portuguese State 105

§1. Portugal as a Unitary State 105

§2. Portugal as a Decentralized, Regionalized, Communitarian and Lusophone State 106

Table of Contents

Chapter 2. The Political and Administrative Organization of the Archipelagos of the Azores and Madeira 108

§1. The Establishment of the Autonomous Regions of the Azores and of Madeira 108

§2. The Regional Organs 110

§3. The Regional Powers 112

Chapter 3. The Sub-State Administrative Organization 114

§1. Administrative Decentralization and the Administrative Function 114

§2. Entities of Portuguese Public Administration 114

§3. The Definition and Status of Local Authorities 115

§4. Types of Local Authorities 119

§5. The Structure of Local Authorities 120

Part IV. The Rights of the Citizens and the Safeguard of the Portuguese Constitution 123

Chapter 1. Fundamental Rights 123

§1. The Relevance of Fundamental Rights in Portugues Constitutional Law 123

§2. Fundamental Rights in the Portuguese Constitution of 1976 124

§3. The General System of Fundamental Rights 125

§4. Rights and Freedoms 126

§5. Economic, Social and Cultural Rights 128

Chapter 2. The Guarantee of the Constitution and the Judicial Review of Constitutionality 129

§1. The Guarantee of the Constitution 129

§2. Constitutional Justice and Judicial Review of Constitutionality 129

Part V. Specific Issues of Portuguese Constitutional Law 131

Chapter 1. Constitutional Exception and Suspension of Fundamental Rights 131

§1. State of Siege and State of Emergency: State of War 131

§2. Fundamental Aspects of the Regime Governing the State of Exception 133

Chapter 2. State and Religion 136

§1. The Importance of Religion to Man and Society 136

§2. The Evolution of Relations Between the State and Religion 137

§3. The Predominance of the Model of Republican Secularism 138

§4. The Evolution of the Relationship Between Portuguese Constitutionalism and Religion 139

§5. The Present Constitutional and Legal System of Cooperative Separation Between State and Religion 141

Selected Bibliography 143

Index 145

List of Abbreviations

CEDH	European Convention on Human Rights
CEU	The European Council
CRP	Constitution of the Portuguese Republic
DUDH	Universal Declaration of Human Rights
LAL	Local Government Act
LLR	Religious Freedom Act
LN	Portuguese Nationality Act
LOG	Portuguese Government Organic Law
LORL	Local Referendum Organic Law
LORR	National Referendum Organic Law
LPP	Political Parties Act
	Law on the regime of the state of siege and the state of emergency
LTC	Constitutional Court Rules of Order
ONU	United Nations Organization
PIDCP	International Covenant on Civil and Political Rights
RAR	Portuguese Parliament's Rules of Order
RCM	Portuguese Council of Ministers' Rules of Order
TCE	The Treaty establishing a Constitution for Europe
TUE	Treaty on European Union (Maastricht Treaty)
UE	European Union

List of Abbreviations

Preface

This work, largely inspired by our *Manual de Direito Constitucional*, aims at describing exhaustively but succinctly the fundamental features of Portuguese Constitutional Law.

It goes without saying that the organization of this monograph, which is a part of the International Encyclopaedia of Constitutional Law, follows closely the rules set out by the publishers, who understandably wish to harmonize the contributions of the various countries. All present similar features and follow a similar pattern.

Jorge Bacelar Gouveia
Lisbon, 1st January 2018

General Introduction

§1. The Birth and Evolution of Portugal

1. Within the European context and even considering the world context, Portugal is one of the oldest existing states. It was founded in the twelfth century, following a certain number of historical facts which jointly gave birth to a new community:

- 1139, the date of the Battle of Ourique, D. Afonso Henriques takes the title of King of Portugal;
- 1143, the date of the Treaty of Zamora, D. Afonso Henriques is recognized as King by D. Afonso VII, King of Castille; and
- 1179, the date of the *Manifestus probatum* edict, Pope Alexander III acknowledges D. Afonso Henriques, who until then had been addressed as duke, as King.

2. Since that founding moment and until the present time, Portuguese history has known many vicissitudes, which can be summarized as follows:

(1) first period, twelfth to fourteenth centuries: territorial consolidation thanks to a succession of conquests and the structuring of institutions according to mediaeval feudal schemes;
(2) second period, fifteenth to sixteenth centuries: the *apogée* of the Portuguese discoveries, with the rounding by Bartolomeu Dias of the Cape of Good Hope (1488), the discovery of the sea route to India by Vasco de Gama (1498) and the discovery of Brazil by Pedro Álvares Cabral (1500);
(3) third period, sixteenth to seventeenth centuries: political submission to Spain between 1580 and 1640, that took the form of a personal union, the crown being worn by the Spanish kings;
(4) fourth period, seventeenth to eighteenth centuries: system of absolute monarchy and decline of the overseas empire as a result of strong competition on the part of other sea powers such as the Netherlands, the United Kingdom and France; and
(5) fifth period, nineteenth to twentieth centuries: inflow and development of Constitutional ideals within the framework of the contemporary State.

3. From the nineteenth century on, Constitutionalism makes its appearance in Portugal. The country is subject to the influences of European and American liberal revolutions. Four different stages may be pointed out, each of which would bring with them differentiated lines and means of evolution:

(1) 1820–1910: the period of royal and liberal Constitutionalism, with three Constitutional texts: the first Constitution in 1822, the Constitutional Charter of 1826 and the Constitution of 1838;
(2) 1910–1926: the period of republican and liberal Constitutionalism, with only one Constitutional text, the Constitution of 1911 (First Republic);
(3) 1926–1974: the period of authoritarian and corporative Constitutionalism, also with only one Constitution, that of 1933 (Second Republic or *Estado Novo*); and
(4) 1974 to present: the period of democratic and social Constitutionalism, which began in 1974 with the 25 April Revolution and was formalized by the Constitution of the Portuguese Republic (CRP) of 2 April 1976, which has been in force since then and has been subject to seven reforms (Third Republic).

4. The present period belongs to the Third Portuguese Republic, which began in 1974, and during which various meaningful economic and social reforms have been undertaken:

- the enactment, since the revolution, of legislation to ensure political democracy through the democratic election of the different ruling bodies and to enable, concomitantly, the dismantling of the former authoritarian structures;
- the granting, in 1975, of independence to those territories that had been until then colonies of Portugal (Angola, on 11 November; Cape Verde, on 5 July; Guinea-Bissau, granted on 24 September 1973, but coming into force only in 1975; Mozambique, on 25 June; and São Tomé and Príncipe, on 12 July);
- Portugal's entry into the European Community on 1 January 1986, at the same time as Spain (it thus became one of twelve Member States);
- in 1989, the economic system started a process of privatization of the many enterprises that had been nationalized in the aftermath of the revolution; and
- in 1999 and 2002, two former Portuguese territories in Asia ceased to belong to Portugal (Macao was integrated into China on 20 December 1999, and East Timor became independent on 20 May 2002, this being the date when independence came into force).

5. Nowadays, Portugal is both continental (it occupies an area of 88,797 square kilometres in the Western part of the Iberian Peninsula), and insular (the groups of islands of the Azores and Madeira, in the Atlantic Ocean, with areas of 2,333 square kilometres and 797 square kilometres respectively). The capital is Lisbon.

According to the 2004 census, the resident population was 10,536,000 and the active population was 5,523,000. This means a population density of fourteen inhabitants/square kilometre.

The major religion is Roman Catholicism, professed by approximately 80% of the population, although many other religions coexist in the country in a context of total religious freedom.

Portugal's currency is the Euro (EU). The GNI *per capita* is EU 12,817.

§2. PORTUGUESE CITIZENSHIP

6. With regard to the human element, the Portuguese State only makes sense if it is based on the group of people who are connected to it by the legal ties of citizenship; that is, the Portuguese citizens.

These ties are a complex legal feature, which reflect multiple and heterogeneous juridical positions that embody a structural relationship of the State as a group of people with a collective destiny and who confer meaning on a political power project.

The rules governing citizenship in Portugal, notwithstanding the relevance of international sources, derive from two main internal sources: on the one hand, the Constitutional norms and principles; on the other, the Portuguese Nationality Act (LN), which sets down the numerous procedures for the granting of citizenship, as well as the effects attached to it.

In what concerns the Constitution, the relevance of Portuguese citizenship as the underlying human component of the State is negligible: the CRP is silent on the subject, it merely states under 'Portuguese citizenship', that 'All persons who are considered as such by law or under an international convention are Portuguese citizens' (Article 4 of the CRP).

7. In the absence of sufficiently dense Constitutional norms, ordinary law has been playing a major role in detailing the criteria that should guide the attribution of citizenship. Thus the LN sets down various modes of acquisition (Articles 1 and following of the LN):

- *original acquisition by birth*, referred to as original citizenship, comprises the cases of birth of Portuguese nationals or of birth on Portuguese soil, albeit with some restrictions;
- *acquisition as a result of an express will*, this mode includes the case of acquisition by minor or mentally incapacitated children whose parents have acquired Portuguese citizenship and the case of acquisition of citizenship by one of the members of a couple (either married or cohabiting couples in *união* de facto);
- *acquisition by adoption*, when the adoptive parents pass on their citizenship to the adopted child; and
- *acquisition by naturalization*, when Portuguese citizenship is conferred on a foreign citizen as a result of substantial ties with Portugal established by residency and knowledge of the country's life.

The Portuguese citizenship ties can be furthermore examined from the perspective of their loss. The LN provides for the renunciation of citizenship, except when this would lead to the status of statelessness.

8. In general there are two main criteria that are usually called upon in order to establish a relationship between a person and a State within the framework of citizenship ties:

(1) *jus sanguinis*; and
(2) *jus soli*.

Jus sanguinis means that citizenship remains in the descending line of those who acquired it at one given time. The citizens of a State are, thus, the descendents of those who were already citizens, aside from the consideration of other criteria.

Conversely, *jus soli* emphasizes the importance of the place of birth of a person. The citizenship of the State, on whose soil birth has taken place, is granted to a person, irrespective of the parents' citizenship.

In practice, these two modes of acquisition cannot operate as such in all their purity and they usually turn into *mixed systems* where both criteria are present although one of them may predominate over the other.

9. A close look at the various modes provided for by the LN for the granting of nationality, where acquisition by birth stands out, emphasizes the predominance of *jus sanguinis* over *jus soli*. The two situations described below illustrate its practical implementation:

(1) The children of a Portuguese father or mother are always Portuguese when born in Portugal and, if born in another country, they are also Portuguese when that father or mother is employed there in the service of the Portuguese government at the time of the birth, if they state that they want to be Portuguese or if they register as such in Portugal.

(2) Children born in Portugal are only Portuguese if they do not hold any other citizenship or if they fall into one of the following categories: 'people born on Portuguese soil to foreign parents, if at least one of the parents was also born here and has his/her residence in Portugal, whether or not he/she is entitled to the right, at the time of the birth'; or 'People born on Portuguese soil to foreign parents who are not serving their government in Portugal at the time of the birth if they state their will to be Portuguese and one of the parents, at the time of the birth, has been legally settled in Portugal for at least five years' (Article 1 of the LN).

§3. Portuguese Sovereignty

10. The structuring functional element of the Portuguese State, concerning the nature of the political power vested upon it, does not allow for doubts when it comes to its sovereign feature.

There are several mentions of it in the CRP where the common notion of the sovereign character of political power, generically represented by the Portuguese Republic in its capacity as a sovereign State based on the sovereignty of the people, is underlined (Articles 1 and ff. of the CRP).

That same conclusion is strengthened by the fundamental option of the Constitution for unitarism as the pattern to be followed when structuring the Portuguese State.

11. From the point of view of the description of the origin of this State power and considering the criterion of its primary nature, it should be noted that there are abundant normative elements in the Constitution that can easily testify to it.

In the first place, the very notion that the Constitutional text is a result of the will of the sovereign people, as is somewhat poetically asserted in the preamble to the

CRP: 'The Constituent Assembly affirms the Portuguese people's decision to defend their national independence.'

Furthermore, the clarity with which it states the principle of constitutionality. For our purpose here, it is not what this means in terms of the hierarchical supremacy of the Constitutional provisions that should concern us, but rather the fact that such statement clearly implies that the Constitution is the founding text of the State's legal order (Article 3 of the CRP).

It should finally also be pointed out the many limitations laid down by the CRP when allowing for the power of revision. There is an extensive clause setting out the material limits to the revision where national independence and the sovereignty of the State's political power are not overseen (Article 288 of the CRP).

12. Considering the two facets of State sovereignty, Portugal is doubly defined as sovereign, both in the internal and in the external order. We shall briefly mention the features that testify to that particular type of political power, the sovereign political power:

- *Internally*, everybody owes allegiance to the State through its Constitution, since the validity of the juridical acts depends on their conformity with the Constitutional text.
- *Externally*, Portugal's international relations must be guided by important principles, one of them being respect for national independence, both its own and that of other states. This principle is asserted when the Constitution establishes the fundamental duties of the State and, more solemnly, when it sets out the material limits to the revision of the Constitution.

13. Moreover the fact that Portuguese sovereignty, both internal and external, is not an obstacle to other modes of political organization also reinforces what has been said on the subject.

Within Portuguese territory, the structuring of sovereign political power operates simultaneously with the acceptance of structures that are endowed with political autonomy but which are not sovereign.

- autonomous regions;
- local government; and
- other administrative bodies.

In international relations, Portuguese sovereignty is compatible with entering into international engagements, as well as with Portugal's membership of various international bodies, which, consequently, project their own juridical orders into the Portuguese juridical order.

§4. The Portuguese Territory

14. With the objective of delineating Portugal's national territory, the CRP dedicates an article to deal with the topic (Article 5 of the CRP), under the title 'Territory'.

According to that provision, the Portuguese territory comprises the three following categories:

(1) land territory;
(2) maritime territory; and
(3) air territory.

15. In what concerns land territory, the CRP deviates from former Constitutional texts and adopts a so-called general clause that avoids mentioning the typology when listing its various component parts.

Moreover, as a result of the conclusion of the decolonization process and of Macao and East Timor drifting out of the Portuguese sphere of influence, the Constitutional provisions, notwithstanding the fact that those territories no longer formally belonged to Portugal, still governed the exercise of some powers with regard to them, became obsolete.

Thus, Portuguese land territory is simultaneously continental and insular:

- *on the European continent* it comprises 'the historically-defined territory' in the Iberian Peninsula; and
- *the insular territory* comprises 'the archipelagos of the Azores and of Madeira'.

Originally a small country, that grew into an immense territorial empire during the discoveries in the sixteenth and seventeenth centuries, Portugal is again confined to a small land territory of approximately 88,000 km^2, whose continental borders, however, are the oldest in Europe.

16. With regard to maritime territory, Portugal, due to its Atlantic position, benefits from a maritime territory that consists of the inshore waters, the territorial sea up to the 12-mile limit and a large continental shelf.

The powers of the Portuguese State over the Atlantic waters, in this case of simple jurisdiction and not of full sovereignty, comprise also the spaces that correspond to the contiguous zone, from 12 to 24 miles beyond the territorial sea, and to the Exclusive Economic Zone (EEZ), up to 200 miles offshore along the mainland coast and around the islands of the archipelagos of the Azores and Madeira, one of the most extensive exclusive economic zones in Europe.

17. Finally, although there is no mention of it in the CRP, Portugal's air territory comprises the airspace on above the land and water territories under State sovereignty and extends vertically up to the lower limit of outer space as defined by international case law.

§5. Shaping and Evolution of the Portuguese Constitution

18. Present Portuguese Constitutional Law rests on the CRP adopted on 2 April 1976, which came into force on 25 April 1976.

This supreme Constitutional Law of the Portuguese State is a corollary of the April 1974 Revolution – the Revolution of the Carnations – which put an end to the nationalist, corporative, fascist-leaning, right-wing and authoritarian regime known as *Estado Novo* that had been strongly influenced by the Italian fascist regime.

PONTEVEDRA
OURENSE
ORENSE
VIANA DO
CASTELO
BRAGA
VILA REAL
Porto
PORTO
N O R T E
ZAMORA
BRAGANÇA
AVEIRO
VISEU
GUARDA
Coimbra
C E N T R O
SALAMANCA
COIMBRA
PORTUGAL
CASTELO BRANCO
LEIRIA
CÁCERES
LISBOA
SANTARÉM
LISBOA
Lisboa
PORTALEGRE
E
EXTREMADURA
ÉVORA
Évora
Mérida
A L E N T E J O
SETÚBAL
BADAJOZ
BEJA
FARO
ALGARVE
Faro
HUELVA
0
100Km

Until the adoption of the CRP, during the two-year interim period, while the democratically elected Constituent Assembly drafted the new Constitution, a series of urgent measures were simultaneously put in place in order to achieve:

- decolonization;
- democratization; and
- development.

19. The CRP text currently contains 296 articles distributed over four parts, some of which comprise chapters. It is preceded by an introduction and has a final part:

- General principles (Articles 1–11).
- Part I – Fundamental rights and duties (Articles 12–79).
- Part II – Economic organization (Articles 80–107).
- Part III – Organization of political power (Articles 108–276).
- Part IV – Protection and Reform of the Constitution (Articles 277–289).
- Final and transitional provisions (Articles 290–296).

20. Since entering into force, the CRP has already undergone seven different reforms, with highly variable scopes and extensions.

The first Constitutional reform of 1982 – Constitution Amendment Act No. 1/1982 – attempted to stabilize the political system. It thus suppressed the Revolution Council, a body composed of military officers, which had been kept by the Constitution as a tribute to the role played by the armed forces in the Revolution of the Carnations. However, the continued existence of an organ of this type gave rise to well-founded doubts about the truly democratic character of the Portuguese State.

The second Constitutional reform of 1989 – Constitution Amendment Act No. 1/1989 – opened the economic system to the large movement of privatization, necessary after Portugal's 1986 entry into the European Community. It repealed the principle of the irreversibility of nationalizations and established the mechanism of political referendum, thus promoting a more participative democracy.

The third Constitutional reform of 1992 – Constitution Amendment Act No. 1/1992 – was specifically aimed at the Constitutional provisions concerning European integration. It ensured that the Maastricht treaty could be ratified without incurring the risk of being ruled unconstitutional and, therefore, made provisions for an enlargement of European integration, allowing for the new common foreign and security policy, the justice and home affairs pillar and the adoption of an economic and monetary union.

The fourth Constitutional reform of 1997 – Constitution Amendment Act No. 1/1997 – did not aim at a specific issue, but included various provisions concerning new fundamental rights, the granting of voting rights in the presidential election to Portuguese citizens living abroad, and the suppression, in peace times, of courts martial, as well as the reinforcement of some of Parliament's legislative powers at the cost of the government's legislative powers.

The fifth Constitutional reform of 2001 – Constitution Amendment Act No. 1/2001 – aimed at preparing the CRP for the ratification of the Rome Statute of the International Criminal Court although it also concerned itself with other matters, such as the possibility for police forces to create trade unions while excluding their right to strike or declaring Portuguese to be the official State language.

The sixth Constitutional reform of 2004 – Constitution Amendment Act No. 1/2004 – modified the regulatory body in charge of the media, enlarged the legislative competencies of the autonomous regions of Azores and Madeira as against the State's legislative competencies and provided for the possibility of setting maximum limits to the number and length of terms in public office, thus bestowing more consistency on the republican principle.

The seventh Constitutional reform of 2005 – Constitution Amendment Act No. 1/2005 – concerned itself exclusively with enabling the holding of direct referendums on international treaties relating to European integration.

§6. The Republican, Democratic and Semi-presidential Political System

21. The republican system was introduced in Portugal in the twentieth century by the Revolution of 5 October 1910. Since then, Portugal has always been a Republic, which means that a president, who is elected to a five-year term of office and who can only be re-elected to an additional single consecutive term, heads the State.

Similarly, public office is generally held on the basis of democratic legitimacy – direct legitimacy in the case of Parliament, and indirect legitimacy in the case of the Government. The Constitution does not recognize any aristocratic privileges and sets out the principle of reappointment, so that no public office can be held for life.

The fact that the State system is a Republic also implies that the Constitution establishes the principle of separation between State and Church. Thus, there is no official religion and all religious faiths must be treated equally; as a result, in various fields, such as the State-held media, the State-run education sector or taxation, religion must be respected in a context of cooperation and not of persecution.

22. Another substantial change directly brought about by the Third Republic has been the development of a democratic system within which different devices for the expression of the people's will coexist, at the three levels of public intervention:

(1) *representative democracy*, asserted in the election by direct universal suffrage of the President of the Republic (five-year term of office), of the members of Parliament (four-year term), of the members of the European Parliament (five-year term), of the members of the regional assemblies (four-year term) and of local authorities (four-year term);
(2) *referendum democracy*, which consists in the possibility of holding referendums at the national, regional and local level on the most relevant issues to be decided upon by their respective governing bodies; and
(3) *participative democracy*, which characterizes the exercise of the various fundamental rights and freedoms of a political nature, conducive to the free formation of public

opinion not only by means of the media, but also by the formation of associations and political parties.

23. The political organs of the Portuguese State comprise the President of the Republic, Parliament (*Assembleia da República*) and the Government, all of which are separate from the judiciary. The above-mentioned political organs share some common powers.

The relationship between these three political organs has been defined according to the *semi-presidential* model, whereby each has effective powers of intervention in political action, grounded in a rationale of separation and interdependence of powers.

The president, who is elected by the people's will, does not hold executive power, and does not even preside over the cabinet (*Conselho de Ministros*), but has the right to intervene in political action under the political powers of his/her office in the following order of increasing weight: (i) power of political veto over legislative acts; (ii) the final power to call political and legislative referendums; (iii) the power to dismiss the Government when the democratic institutions are not functioning regularly; and (iv) the power to dissolve Parliament [*Assembleia da República*].

Parliament is unicameral. It has 230 members, elected to a four-year term in accordance with the system of proportional representation using the d'Hondt method of highest average. There are twenty constituencies on national territory (eighteen districts and two autonomous regions) and another two for Portuguese citizens residing in foreign countries (one for Europe and one for outside Europe). Parliament exercises the most important legislative powers, including that of amending the Constitution. The formation of the Government originates in Parliament since the government is accountable to Parliament.

The members of the Government are appointed by the Head of State following the results of a general election. It is the organ that conducts the general government of the country, with a few legislative and political powers, and, above all, with very wide administrative powers. The Government comprises the prime minister and a variable number of ministers depending on the departments represented in it, as well as secretaries of State. It is the supreme organ of the State's Civil Service.

Despite those traits that characterize the Portuguese political system as being semi-presidential, practice has emphasized the predominance of Parliament. This is very much the result of the fact that, over the past ten years, the same ideology has held both a majority in Parliament and the office of Head of State. It should also be pointed out that parliamentary composition, even during 2002–2005, when there was a period of political cohabitation, always enabled the formation of stable government majorities, an important political factor in emphasizing the parliamentary side of any semi-presidential regime.

§7. Unitarian Structure of the Portuguese State and Minor Political Entities

24. The territorial organization of the Portuguese State is not completely centralized despite the fact that Portugal is a Unitarian State, where no other state political structures exist apart from the ones mentioned above. This is a firm position held by Portuguese Constitutionalism practically from the first, and certainly influenced by the exiguity of its territory.

Within its territory, the State recognizes decentralized political structures with the ensuing related powers:

- political and legislative powers in the case of the autonomous regions of the Azores and Madeira; and
- administrative powers in the case of administrative bodies, chiefly local authorities.

25. The autonomous regions of the Azores and Madeira – one for each of those groups of islands in the North Atlantic – are bodies that find their definition in the CRP. Beside administrative powers, they also hold political and legislative powers for reasons that stem from the need to overcome the difficulties of collective organization on islands. Their insular position requires a larger amount of political and legislative self-government albeit with due respect to the unity of the Portuguese Republic.

From the legislative viewpoint, the powers of the autonomous regions are quite extensive; they are entitled to issue regional legislative decrees for their territories, unless the subject matter does not come within their powers or falls within the exclusive powers of Parliament (in some cases, however, these may be delegated).

The organization of the autonomous regions comprises its own organs, which are the legislative assemblies, elected in the regional territory by direct universal suffrage of the Portuguese citizens who inhabit it, and the Regional Governments, appointed in the wake of the electoral results, which are the regional executive, accountable to the legislative assemblies.

The State's representation in each of the autonomous regions falls to the Representative of the Republic, a single-member body appointed by the President of the Republic, with limited powers of intervention in the Regional Government system, comprising little more than the signing of regional decrees and the power to bring them before the Constitutional Court for judicial review.

26. Another significant dimension of the territorial organization of the Portuguese State is found in local government.

Local Authorities are bodies of local self-government with administrative powers, present at two different levels:

(1) the municipal level, where there are a total of 308 municipal authorities on the continent and in the islands. Their organs are the municipal assembly (*assembleia municipal*) and the municipal executive (*câmara municipal*), both democratically elected by the citizens who reside within the area of each municipality (*concelho*);
(2) the parish level, with 3,092 parishes, similarly scattered over the whole territory. Their organs are the parish assembly and the parish executive (*junta de freguesia*), the first being also democratically elected by the citizens who reside within the area of each parish.

Part I. Sources of Portuguese Law

Chapter 1. The Constitution as the Main Source of Portuguese Constitutional Law

§1. General Meaning of Constitution

27. The Constitution, being the *lex suprema* of the State, is the legislative source that contains the system of norms and legal principles, which lay down the basic structure of the State at the supreme level of the positive legal system:

- *of the State as power*, organizing its organs and their own powers, as well as defining the status of their members; and
- *of the State as community*, establishing the relationship between institutional public power and the citizens, who are its underlying human component.

It should not be assumed, however, that the contemporary meaning of Constitution is entirely new. There are multiple previous examples, albeit used from a purely institutional perspective.

28. One of these examples is the pioneering case of Aristotle, who in his *Politics* defined the notion of Constitution as *Politeia*, thereby meaning that a Constitution is the arrangement of magistracies in a State, especially of the highest of all, and who further included in it the purpose of the political community: 'The government is everywhere sovereign in the State, and the Constitution is in fact the government'.

This concept of Constitution, like that of the *rem publicam constituere* of the Roman State, had nothing in common with what would become the present concept of Constitution. It has its place within the rationale of the institutional notion of Constitution present in every State alongside the notions of *nomos*, or law, and *psefisma*, or decree.

It was during the Middle Ages that the embryo of a notion closer to the present concept of Constitution emerged, namely the notion of the unifying and superior order of the State.

29. The Constitution – in this sense – is a public power act vested with maximum supremacy in the State's legal order, which establishes the structure of its social, economic and political systems.

That is why it is appropriate to emphasize within the concept of Constitution some elements that are congenital, thus making it easier to distinguish it from other concepts:

- *the subjective element* – an intentional act of the State that does not possess the nature of custom and belongs in the category of voluntary sources of law;
- *the formal element* – occupies the highest place in the State's legal order; and
- *the material element* – regulates the main choices of the State with regard to social, economic and political systems.

30. When considering these defining elements, it is simultaneously possible to approach the Constitution from a variety of angles owing to the four perspectives that it may comprise and that should be referred to as its dimensions or meanings:

(1) *A material dimension*: the material Constitution, in the choices it makes and provides for, expresses a given content; ideologically born in the era of liberalism, the evolution of the Constitutional State has been widening that content and has, above all, introduced a degree of relativization.
(2) *A formal dimension*: the formal Constitution expresses the notion of a legislative act that takes a supreme position in positive law.
(3) *A textual (or instrumental) dimension*: the written Constitution is seen as a legislative act, which operates the codification of a given branch of law, laying down, in a scientific and systematic arrangement, its fundamental rules.
(4) *An institutional dimension*: the institutional Constitution reflects a minimum desire to organize the State, independently from the character the latter may have as a result of options concerning its contents, form or hierarchical location.

§2. The Constitution as Law of the State

31. After having examined the general sense of the concept of Constitution and the various elements pertaining to it, as well as the meanings and modalities into which it divides itself, we come to the conclusion that the first distinguishing feature of the Constitution lies in its nature as law of the State.

As a matter of fact this is the trait that contributes foremost to the individualization of the Constitution within the context of liberalism and of the historical affirmation of the rule of law.

This is also the characteristic that better helps place the Constitution within the general theory of law with regard to its sources, interpretation and enforcement.

32. The Constitution shows in the first place a legal facet since, as a source of law, namely of Constitutional Law, it is part of the larger framework of law.

This means that the Constitution represents a wilfully directed normative system and gives expression to a specific will, rather than arising out of social spontaneity.

However, it should not be assumed that custom is incompatible with Constitutional regulation or even that a mixed Constitutional system, containing both legal and customary rules, is not feasible.

Incompatibility is one thing; another is the demand that the Constitutional text be framed in the context of a legislative act with all the associated characteristics.

33. In spite of being a law of the State, the Constitution is not a usual, ordinary law. It flows from the power of the State as the paramount expression of public power represented in the State by way of its internal sovereignty.

This fact ensures a clear distinction between truly Constitutional texts and other texts, eventually even those bearing the name of 'Constitution', but which, to speak the truth, do not possess any of the Constitution's defining features.

We have here in mind the so-called European Constitution, which is no more than an international treaty, of the institutional category, but which has been repeatedly called 'Constitutional'. The fact is, however, that the UE it proposes to govern is neither a State and nor does it have constituent power of its own – it is merely the creation of the states that have formed it into a structure similar to a confederation.

§3. The Constitution as the Supreme Act of Public Law

34. The Constitution is also a particular type of law due to its position at the top of the legal order; it occupies the summit of the pyramid as Hans Kelsen metaphorically said.

The formal hierarchical supremacy of the Constitution within the legal order of the State to which it belongs is embodied in three main features:

(1) the principle of constitutionality;
(2) the devaluation of conflicting public legal acts; and
(3) the responsibility for Constitutional breaches.

35. The *principle of constitutionality* by placing the Constitution above all other sources, rules or legal principles is the substantive aspect of Constitutional supremacy. Its purpose is to assert that there is a hierarchy in the legal order and that all other sources and acts without Constitutional significance must respect it.

Should those acts, sources, norms or principles conflict with the Constitution, it follows that they are *unconstitutional* on grounds of infringement of the said pattern with which they must comply.

And this supremacy, contained in the principle of constitutionality, is wide-ranging because it is both:

(1) supremacy with regard to acts of public law; and
(2) supremacy with regard to behaviours of a public law nature.

36. Hence the consequences, when setting out its effects aimed at repressing breaches of that supremacy, cannot but be considerable.

If that were not the case and the adjective aspect did not operate, we would be faced with a norm without sanction. For the Constitution, being as a result an imperfect law, it would be difficult for it to keep its status of normative and positive supremacy.

From a practical viewpoint the sanction provided by the principle of constitutionality has two distinct aspects, which may even overlap and whose purpose it is to repress unconstitutional acts and behaviours:

(1) the devaluation of unconstitutional legal acts through their suppression from the legal order; and
(2) the responsibility of the authors of unconstitutional behaviour through the implementation of the various legal responsibility mechanisms.

§4. The Constitution as the Core of the Positive Legal Order

37. Having the Constitution as the *core law* also means that its contents – not its legal structure or supreme force – assume the highest conceivable relevance in the role that a legal act is meant to play: to be the core of the legal order.

This core position of the Constitution implies that its provisions shall lay down the main choices of the life organized within the State and, due to their importance, contained in the Constitutional text.

As a result, the centrality of the Constitution may be examined from a double perspective:

(1) either as a *qualitative centrality* since the Constitution contains the essential lines that should guide life in the community and inside the State apparel; and
(2) or as a *quantitative centrality* since the Constitution, in view of the fact that not everything is constitutionally relevant, includes the main choices, even though other aspects may be left to lower levels of the legal order.

38. Nevertheless, it cannot be disguised that the definition of 'Constitutional matters'– that is, of the norms and principles that should be placed at the Constitutional level – is deeply complex.

Starting from the notions of formal Constitution and material Constitution, it is with respect to these that a division is drawn between two sorts of norms or Constitutional principles:

(1) *constitutional norms and principles* which embody matters that have the dignity of the Constitution and are, therefore, materially Constitutional; and
(2) *constitutional norms and principles* vested with Constitutional force of a supreme nature and, consequently, formally Constitutional.

There is no doubt, with regard to some of the matters that they belong in the Constitution as a result of their obvious Constitutional nature, inherent to the very concept and functions of a Constitutional text, which is to lay down the foundation of the State and its legal order.

In such cases, it is perfectly normal that Constitutional norms and principles, which are 'materially' Constitutional on account of the matters they deal with, should also be 'formally' Constitutional. The form being at the service of the content, they are, therefore, under the special protection afforded by the Constitution.

39. In practice the above is not always true and there may exist some dubious situations, when it is difficult to determine whether or not the norms and principles at issue are Constitutional from the material point of view.

Thus, from the perspective of their contents and Constitutional location, sometimes the 'material' and the 'formal' Constitutional norms and principles instead of overlapping completely, as they should, do so only in part. The relationship between them is like that of properly intersecting circles; they only touch in part. Consequently, there are:

- norms and principles, the subject matter of which is Constitutional but that, nevertheless, are not formally considered as such; and
- norms and principles, the subject matter of which is not Constitutional but which are, nevertheless, formally considered as such.

This is not a desirable situation since it compromises the perfect symbiosis that the Constitution should present, a coin with a face and a reverse, where one of the two cannot exist without the other.

§5. The Constitution as Legal Code

40. The Constitution, in its quality as legal act, is also intended as a codification of the branch of law that deals with it, that is, as a *code of Constitutional Law.*

To tell the truth, whether now or in the past, that name has never been applied to it. However, it is also true that Constitutions have probably been one of the first manifestations of the tendency towards codifying laws.

The issue is purely one of terminology; it is not substantive. Constitutions, whatever their name, are real codes in the technical and scientific sense of the term.

41. The rationale behind the assertion that the concept of code is appropriate when referring to the Constitution is based on the fact that states concentrate in their Constitutional texts the whole set of rules and principles that deal with their positive Constitutional Law and do it in a systematic, synthetic and scientific manner:

- *systematically* because the norms and principles are structured according to uniform patterns, without duplications or obvious loopholes;
- *synthetically* because the Constitutional precepts are always selective when setting out their provisions, leaving certain details that would not make sense in a Constitutional context to other levels of legislation; and
- *scientifically* because the organization of the Constitutional matters is in accordance with scientific principles of a logical nature, which result in a coherent system of solutions.

Even if all the requisites for a law code were not met, obvious historic reasons for that definition could be pointed out: Constitutionalism, with its well-known contribution to the framing of Constitutions, also fought against absolute monarchies with their ingrained uncertainty in terms of rules, evident in capriciously enacted and revoked laws, in customary norms difficult to locate and in the immense vacua left to the arbitrary decision of the public powers of the time.

42. However, the mere existence of a code – in this case a Constitutional code bearing the name of 'Constitution'– does not always signify that it comprises the whole of the Constitutional principles and norms belonging to a given positive Constitutional Law.

This is why the hypothesis of the existence of *extravagantes* arises, which in spite of having Constitutional significance or dealing with Constitutional matters, did not manage to gain entry into the Constitution, taken here in its documentary sense.

The *documentary Constitution is, thus, the Constitutional statute that codifies Constitutional Law* even though it does not bear such denomination and is not expected to comprise all the norms and principles that are considered to be Constitutional.

Several reasons may be at the root of the emergence of Constitutional statutes and principles outside the Constitution:

- *the original extravagantes*, that is, Constitutional norms and principles, which at the outset, when the Constitution came into force, were not enshrined in it intentionally because they dealt with matters that were deserving of an autonomous and specific handling; and
- *the subsequent extravagantes*, that is, Constitutional norms and principles, which were laid down later, within the context of subsequent Constitutional vicissitudes not conducive to their incorporation into the Constitutional text.

43. This means that there is a *Constitutional Law outside the Constitution, embodied in the set of legal acts, norms and principles that are not comprised in the canonical text, the latter being understood as the codifying law of this legal branch.*

When examining this Constitution outside the Constitution, a task is unavoidable considering the centrality of this fundamental law, we may follow two separate schemes:

(1) *the material 'outside' Constitutional Law (Direito Constitucional Extravagante Material)* comprising the legal acts, norms and principles that belong within the material Constitution but neither to the documentary Constitution, nor, usually, the formal Constitution. Their value is merely sub-Constitutional and they are enshrined in a piecemeal manner; and

(2) *the formal 'outside' Constitutional Law (Direito Constitucional Extravagante Formal)* consisting of the legal acts, norms and principles located in the formal Constitution and possessing supreme Constitutional significance but that are not found in the documentary Constitution.

44. The CRP is a living example of how these two modalities of 'outside' Constitutional Law may be implemented.

The highest number of cases is to be found within *the material 'outside' Constitutional Law*; one only has to think of the copious legislation with sub-Constitutional significance relating to Constitutional matters that completes or applies the choices made by the formal documentary Constitution:

- *Rules of Order of the Assembly of the Republic* (RAR): a political act adopted under the form of a resolution, which details the procedures followed in the organization and operation of the Assembly of the Republic, executing and applying many of the norms and principles of the CRP.
- *Constitutional Court Rules of Order* (LTC): a legislative act that sets out the organization and operation of and the procedures followed by the Constitutional Court, the main body of the Constitutional review system.
- *Electoral laws*: legislative acts dealing with the elections, establishing their various stages and the criteria underlying the choice of the candidates according to the bodies for which they are passed.
- *National Referendum Act* (LORR): a legislative act, which stipulates the conditions under which national referendums shall be held, the procedure to be followed thereby and the effects their outcome might have on the actions of the organs of government.
- *Political Parties Act* (LPP): a legislative act that establishes the rules and regulations governing the foundation and extinction of political parties, their structures and the relationships between their members.

45. As stated previously, there is also *a formal 'outside' Constitutional Law*, whereby we mean legal acts dealing with Constitutional matters that acquire the same significance as the formal Constitution in spite of being located outside the canonical text of the Constitution.

These are the cases where the theory of Constitutional Law has detected 'communications' between the Constitutional and sub-Constitutional sources that enable the latter to gain the same status as the first through a process of 'constitutionalization'. This can take the form of either a formal or a material incorporation. The examples therefore are numerous:

- *the national symbols, the national flag* and the *national anthem*, which were adopted by decree of the Constituent Assembly of the First Republic and are deemed to have Constitutional significance;
- *the Universal Declaration of Human Rights* (DUDH), the reference whenever the system of human right has to be construed or extended;
- *the so-called open-ended clause of atypical fundamental rights*, which enables the catalogue of human rights to be enriched through the addition of rights derived from non-Constitutional sources; and
- *the cooperative principles*, which are established externally in the doctrinal texts of cooperativism.

Chapter 2. Constituent Power and Constitutional Reform

§1. Constituent Power and the Birth of the Constitution

46. The Constitution as a human phenomenon and, particularly, as a lawmaking act can be examined under a *dynamic aspect* that considers the concrete possibilities of the vital moments of its birth.

The starting point is the fundamental notion that the Constitution, in its quality as legal act, should be viewed in its peculiarity since it reflects not only norms and principles, but also a range of choices that mark it indelibly as the product of a particular will to structure the State and society.

We shall now endeavour to understand the fundamental aspects that define the circumstances in which the Constitution emerges as a legal act, that is, the theory of Constituent Power as developed by Emmanuel Sieyès.

47. The birth of a new Constitution is brought about by the eruption of constituent power, that is, the power that translates at any given moment the unending possibility the State has to organize itself, a power that never disappears but remains latent – like a 'dormant volcano' – in non-constituent periods (of volcanic non-activity), and all the other powers flow from it.

Constituent power – which simply consists in the framing of a new Constitution – goes through different stages and has distinct scopes depending on the real-life circumstances surrounding its emergence. It may be an *initial constituent power*, when it is exercised for the first time, or a *subsequent constituent power*, when it has already been exercised: the power is initial when the State also makes its own appearance at that time and gives itself a Constitution, as is the case after a country has gained independence; it is subsequent when a new Constitution abrogates an older one and simply replaces it.

A third alternative exists, although nowadays it may be considered ancient history: when the birth of the Constitution does not occur at the foundational moment of the State but, simultaneously, no revocation of a former Constitutional order takes place, as was the case during liberalism, when the first written Constitutions made their appearance putting an end to the order of the *Ancien Régime* and gradually replaced it with the Constitutional order of the contemporary State.

48. Constituent power, under that self-organizing aspect, takes on an umbilical relationship with the entity entrusted with it, that is, the State structure.

There is no constituent power outside the State as there is no Constitution outside the State, no matter how distinct the denominations and concepts might be.

On the contrary, the manifestation of a constituent power enabling the State to exercise at any time its supreme power of self-organization as a competence of competences (*Kompetenz-Kompetenz*) is one of its essential elements.

§2. The Characteristic Features of Constituent Power

49. If the notion of constituent power has become as relevant as that of the Constitution, it is greatly the result of the work of Emmanuel Sieyès, its first theoretician.

Yet, practically from the start, the question arose of the definition of its characteristic features. Three aspects were deemed fundamental:

(1) *originality* – it should be an original power, not preceded by any other power;
(2) *independence* – it should be a power at the summit of the hierarchy and not subordinate to any other power; and
(3) *absolute nature* – it should be a power with no material limits, not subject to any other norm or parameter.

These were to become the traits distinguishing constituent power from other powers of the State that have other distinctive features, which, for their part, denote their minority with regard to constituent power, the power of powers.

50. However, the foregoing notion has become obsolete since constituent power has been compelled gradually to absorb the demands of the rule of law to which it owes its existence. Nowadays, on the contrary, constituent power is:

- democratically legitimized;
- materially limited; and
- inserted in a given cultural background.

51. The constituent power, as the supreme power of the State, will never be able to escape the demands of people's sovereignty and democratic legitimacy. If there is a power that must be democratic, then it is in the first place constituent power.

The question of who holds constituent power is evidently a question that cannot be dissociated from the general conception of political power, which is inherently wielded by the State and other structures that exercise that type of power.

It is equally true that the assertion made by Constitutionalism of the dualism *constituent power versus constituted power* rested from the beginning on a democratic concept, of the contractual type, originating both in John Locke and in Jean-Jacques Rousseau. For John Locke, supreme power rests with the people; for Jean-Jacques Rousseau, more radically, the general will of the majority was the exclusive holder of constituent power.

52. Another notion that was soon to be mitigated concerns the alleged absolute quality of constituent power.

As the State power that it is, constituent power cannot have an unlimited capacity to regulate by law. It is subject, like the other powers, albeit to a lesser degree, to the limitation of barriers set in the name of principles and values of a transpositive character that the constituent power must respect.

This is the same as saying that constituent power is bound by several limits on its course towards the expansion of the vast public power it holds in its capacity as the positive power that it is and will never cease to be. These limits may fall into various categories:

- *transpositive limits*, connected with the legitimacy of the law in general and with pursuing justice (natural law);
- *structural positive limits* that concern the structure of the composite State where the federated states must submit, in the framing of their respective Constitutions, to the limits established by the federal Constitution although, for their part, they are entitled to add other limits of their own; and
- *positive procedural limits* associated with the expression in concrete of each constituent moment along the path towards the definitive framing of a Constitutional text.

53. Moreover it should not be forgotten that constituent power, since it is the power of a State in concrete, should allow the peculiarities of the community of people that wield it to come through. This power – like the law in general – cannot but reflect the fundamental choices of the State and the people it concerns.

It must, therefore, prove adaptable, through the finding of new expressions, to the changes that might be, at any given time, democratically decreed, and, hence, occupy a place in the sphere of culture of the law in general, which is also undoubtedly inherent to Constitutional Law.

§3. Particular Manifestations of the Constituent Power

54. Having examined the general characteristics that define the constituent power as the most important power of the State, the moment has come to describe the possible modes in which it expresses itself.

In conceptual terms, the constituent power translates itself in the framing of a new Constitution, the supreme legal act of the State, endowed with its own identity within the organization of the State.

The constituent power should, consequently, not be confounded with other realities, which are also globally Constitutional but where no change of the Constitution and its main features occur.

55. From the theoretical viewpoint, there are three different modes of exercising the constituent power – *as total constitutional vicissitudes* – that evidence the birth of a new Constitutional order:

(1) *constitutional independence*: the political creation of a State, with which the proclamation of its first Constitution is associated;
(2) *constitutional revolution*: a change in the notion of law as a result of new Constitutional options. It takes place, both materially and formally, against the former Constitutional order; and
(3) *constitutional transition*: a change in the law project and its essential Constitutional options, nevertheless respecting entirely the former formal Constitution by using the forms of production of that normative will as if conducting a reform of the Constitution.

56. With regard to the procedure, a distinction should be made between two notions that are found in the expression of constituent power:

(1) *material constituent power*; and
(2) *formal constituent power*.

The material constituent power reflects the options with regard to the content, which express the new Constitutional order that shall be established following the new law project developed in opposition to the pre-existing one. Thus the new notion pervades the whole legal order.

The formal constituent power represents the formalization of the mentioned content by means of the framing of the Constitution and of the constituent acts by which it is enacted.

There is, of course, a relationship of subordination between the formal constituent power and the material Constitutional power, the first being subordinate to the latter. It would not be admissible to see the result of the new concept of law being countered by the formal result of the subsequently adopted written Constitution.

§4. Constitutional Reform

57. More than with respect to any other vicissitude of the Constitution, be it far-reaching or otherwise, special attention should be paid, on both theoretical and phenomenological grounds, to the *reform (revision) of the Constitution*, which expresses itself in the framing of a law of reform enacted through its own particular procedure.

Constitutional reform, based on the corresponding power of reform, consists in the possibility of altering the originally established Constitutional order, but only at a secondary level since it is restricted both by the fundamental options of the original Constitution and by the provisions of the strict legislative procedure that has been laid down for that purpose.

In other words, since the constituent power at work in a Constitutional reform is the original power, it cannot be confounded with the total Constitutional vicissitudes that reflect the birth of a new Constitution, such as Constitutional revolution or transition.

It happens sometimes that the constituent power takes the appearance of a Constitutional reform – as is almost always the case when there is a Constitutional transition – and implies, therefore, a total Constitutional experience. In those circumstances, it is evidently not the name that counts but rather the underlying conceptual reality, which derives from a hidden but nonetheless genuine constituent power that is always original.

58. The Constitutional reform takes form through the enactment of a Constitutional Law containing provisions that establish a connection with the existing text of the Constitution. The following are its effects:

- *revoking effect*: the former Constitutional precept is repealed;
- *innovative effect*: a new precept is added;

- *modifying effect*: the existing Constitutional precept is given a new normative formulation; and
- *suspensive effect*: the existing Constitutional precept ceases to be in force during a given period of time.

59. The functions that are normally conferred on the Constitutional reform process flow from the realism it translates with regard to the ever difficult and, above all, unstable relationship between Constitutional Law and Constitutional reality since that body of rules and principles is called upon to reflect at all times the evolution of the politico-social situation and must simultaneously command it.

The result is a compromise, admitting, up to a certain point, the adaptation of the Constitutional order to the changes occurring in the Constitutional reality. This causes the Constitution to be better suited to that same reality, while taking care that its fundamental singularity, on which its notion of law is built, is preserved.

Should there be no provision for Constitutional reform, the original form of the Constitution would probably be maintained for a longer period. However, another highly probable consequence would be for that version of the Constitution, unable to change owing to its rigidity – which would deprive it of the necessary security valve allowing the existing Constitutional system to be maintained – to end up detonating violent mechanisms of alteration of the Constitutional order that would open the door to a new Constitution.

In short, it can be said that Constitutional reform discharges some of the following important tasks:

- *to update the constitutional order*, adapting it to the Constitutional circumstances in view of newly felt needs and concerns, and altering some of its options;
- *to interpret the constitutional order*, setting out new hermeneutical criteria with regard to unclarified points, which, quite often, only Constitutional practice can detect; and
- *to complete the constitutional order*, filling in loopholes and correcting mistakes in the current provisions, in addition to incorporating new instruments.

60. A closer look at the provisions governing the process of Constitutional reform, from the perspective of the rules that set out the parallel legislative procedure, leads to the conclusion that there are *exceptional and special rules*, which diverge to a greater or lesser degree from those under which the ordinary legislative process is conducted.

Constitutional Law theory has identified five large classes of rules gathered under the denomination 'limits of constitutional reform' on the grounds that they owe their existence to the need to restrain the breadth usually associated with ordinary legislative power, yet are not desirable, in such large-scale, in the lawmaking process of Constitutional reform.

This is the sense and the scope of the above-mentioned limits to Constitutional reform:

- *organic limits*: rules that lay down which organ is vested with the exclusive power of Constitutional reform, within the general distribution of legislative power among the organs of government;
- *temporal limits*: rules that prevent the exercise of the power of amendment at all times, only admitting its periodical occurrence;
- *procedural limits*: rules that lay down particular requirements for the procedure to be used when amending the Constitution, which increase its difficulty, such as the usually required aggravated majorities;
- *circumstantial limits*: rules that deny the expression of the power of Constitutional reform in times of grave emergency, when there is a situation of Constitutional exception; and
- *material limits*: rules that entrench a certain number of matters, values, principles or devices that are at the core of the conception of law embodied in the written Constitution, the suppression of which would put that conception in jeopardy.

§5. Entrenched Matters and Constitutional Reform

61. We shall deal here more in detail with the matters that, owing to their practical relevance and theoretical complexity, constitute limits to the reform of the Constitution, thus raising the question of whether and how far it is possible to abide by them.

The limits on the matters susceptible to constitutional reform are finally, as astonishing as it may seem, the most obvious restrictions connected with the expression of the power of reform of the Constitution, since they are the attestation of the limits inherent in the concept of constitutional reform.

If they had not been conceived, some kind of juridical and Constitutional phenomenon would certainly exist, yet the reform of the Constitution would never take place.

The question, therefore, lays in defining those matters considering that the written Constitution entrenches them *in express provisions setting limits to the reform of the Constitution*; this, in turn, raises two other kinds of issues:

(1) *the issue of the binding force of said provisions* as compared with other Constitutional precepts; and
(2) *the issue of the definition of the limits of Constitutional reform* comprised in said provisions – considering that the latter enjoy different degrees of intensity – so that it may result clearly therefrom, should the relevant provision be infringed, in what is effectively an entrenched matter.

62. With regard to the first issue, there has been much dispute around the legal force of the Constitutional precepts that lay down provisions for entrenching some matters in the Constitution. A dispute that may extend to all the other provisions issued by the (original) constituent power that embodies the exercise of the power of reform; the question, therefore, is not confined to the matters that are entrenched, but also arises with regard to all the other remaining limits.

Basically, there are three possible positions concerning the eventual alteration of the mentioned provisions, when amending the Constitution, should the need arise to dispose of those limits and amend matters that had been until then protected by them:

(1) *The theory of the impossibility of reform*: according to this theory, in view of the fact that the provisions for Constitutional reform have been enacted by the original constituent power, only a new manifestation of the same original constituent power could modify or eliminate them; it could never be achieved by a Constitutional Amendment Act, which is always, in relation to the former a constituted and not a constituent power.
(2) *The theory of revisability*: according to this theory, the provisions concerning Constitutional reform do not carry more force than any other Constitutional precept; if the Constitution, in its original version, provides for the power of Constitutional reform, it ensues that that same power may be exercised over the regime governing Constitutional reform and, therefore, that the contents of such provisions may also be amended.
(3) *The theory of the double reform* (or phased reform): in this perspective the amendment of matters entrenched under the Constitutional reform provisions – predominantly, but not exclusively material limits – must occur in two stages: first, the provision that entrenches the matter at issue is eliminated and it is only at a later stage, in the course of another Constitutional reform procedure, that the device or the principle no longer protected by the meanwhile repealed entrenchment provision may be suppressed.

We support the first theory of the entrenchment of the provisions that establish limits on the matters susceptible to Constitutional reform, thereby following the rationale of maintaining the utmost respect for the will of the constituent power. We cannot conceive that, after the enactment by the constituent power of a whole set of provisions meant to be more enduring than the others, the power of Constitutional reform, created and enabled by that same constituent power, may surge and adulterate the initial will. The creation shall never surpass the creator!

63. But will this conclusion not lead to the drastic practical consequences of an excessive rigidity of Constitutional systems, since the possibility of amending the Constitutional order is thereby denied to the coming generations? Our reply to that question, raised from a functional standpoint or even from the perspective of legitimacy, is a firm 'no'.

The enshrinement in the written Constitution itself of a mechanism for amending the Constitution is a clear sign, in view of the functions conferred upon it, that a door was left open with the intention of enabling the Constitutional system to be perfected and the accompaniment of the evolution of Constitutional real-life circumstances.

It is clear that the issue takes on another, much larger dimension from the moment that the objective is no longer just a Constitutional reform but something more, such as a radical change of the Constitutional order. In that case, since technically a Constitutional reform is not viable, a Constitutional revolution will take place.

Whatever the case, the original constituent power remains and it can never be prevented from framing a new Constitution should that be the will of the State, expressed in accordance with the existing Constitutional schemes of effectiveness. It is most important not to confuse names and to recognize when a rupture of the Constitutional order occurs and the latter is to be replaced by a new one. The constituent power itself remains untouched, waiting for a new opportunity to express itself.

64. Now that the Constitutional normative force of the provisions that assert the limits of Constitutional reform have been clarified, we should analyse, in response to the other question raised previously, various circumstances where those very provisions are infringed in order to understand the consequences of this fact.

We should be aware, however, that the Constitutional texts do not always apply correctly the concept of limits of Constitutional reform, bestowing that name on matters that may not deserve to occupy such an elevated positions in the context of the written Constitution.

A hermeneutical task of the greatest difficulty is, hence, necessary to determine which are the fundamental principles and the choices that have structured the birth of a new constituent power.

The entrenchment of certain matters, although assisted by the express provisions laying them down, derives from the essence of the concept of law enshrined in the Constitutional order.

65. And what happens when certain matters have been entrenched but, in reality, do not fit into that concept, the constituent power having mistakenly classified them as such? In other words, what happens when the provisions concerning the limits of Constitutional reform are not respected because they are excessive?

The answer depends on whether the entrenchment provisions grant or do not grant cast-iron protection to the above-mentioned matters. Four distinct instances may be referred to, where the total or partial inexistence of such provisions is considered:

- *There are no entrenchment provisions*: if the matter is not of core significance, a normal Constitutional reform will take place; if the matter is deemed to belong to the fundamental core of the Constitution (*Verfassungskern*), even if a Constitutional reform in a formal sense takes place, what actually occurs is a *Constitutional transition* since a new Constitutional order is born as a result of the adulteration of that core.
- *There are entrenchment provisions*: if the matter is not of core significance and the provision mistakenly refers to a matter that does not attain such dimension, then *a non-revolutionary rupture* occurs as a consequence of the formal breach of said provision, albeit without affecting the identity of the Constitution – the act only survives if it achieves Constitutional effectiveness; if the matter is of core significance, a *Constitutional revolution* takes place since the identity of the Constitution has been breached and, simultaneously, the formal compliance with the Constitution of the admissible amendments to the Constitutional text has been disrupted.

66. Finally there is a particular situation that must be distinguished from all the foregoing cases: *the linguistic modification – albeit not prescriptive – of the provisions regarding Constitutional reform.*

The continuity we advocate is not of style but rather of the Constitutional order, and, therefore, merely linguistic changes, when their meaning does not affect that order, have no effect on the validity of the Constitutional reform.

§6. The Hyper-rigidity of the Portuguese Constitution

67. The Portuguese Constitutional experience, in what concerns Constitutional reform, is extremely rich – not only because the regime of Constitutional reform is dense, but also on account of some interesting occurrences, at the border between obeisance and breach of its rules. The CRP dedicates to this question Chapter 2 of Part IV of its text.

Indeed such systematic importance is well attuned to the value bestowed on it by doctrinal opinion, although the practical relevance of the fact is scarce. When the CRP first came into force, one of the most discussed topics was the issue of the entrenched matters.

68. The CRP is actually a good example of a highly rigid Constitution, since the procedure for amendment, following a rationale that seeks to protect its stability as demanded by its legitimating function of the Portuguese legal system, sets down numerous limits that restrict the power to amend it:

- *organic limits*: among the legislative bodies, only Parliament can approve a Constitutional reform;
- *time limits*: the Constitutional amendment procedure can only take place every five years (ordinary reform), although a Constitutional amendment procedure can be initiated at any time as long as it is supported in Parliament by a majority of four-fifths of its absolute number of members;
- *procedural limits*: the legislative procedure for Constitutional reform is subject to a few peculiar requirements, such as the fact that it can only be initiated by Parliament, that it must be adopted by a supermajority of two-thirds of its members entitled to vote, and that the President of the Republic shall not refuse to promulgate it;
- *material limits*: a considerable number of matters as defined in the original version of the CRP cannot be subjected to amendment; these subject matters are considered the identifying traits that characterize the CRP's notion of law; and
- *circumstantial limits*: Constitutional reform cannot be initiated or approved during exceptional circumstances, that is during a state of siege or a state of emergency declared in accordance with the Constitution.

Chapter 3. The Secondary Sources of Portuguese Constitutional Law

§1. The Diminished Relevance of Constitutional Custom

69. The notion of Constitution, not only when it was born but throughout its subsequent life, is inevitably associated with its legal source in view of the fact that it translates normative options created for the purpose of fixing the status of political power and its relationship with the citizens.

It is indeed a fact that the legal source is not the sole possible source of law; hence, we are fully justified in examining, as well, the relevance that may be attributed to other normative sources following the way this issue is dealt with in the General Theory of Law.

At this point, our aim is to appreciate the legal relevance of *Constitutional custom* that is the customary rules that affect the Constitutional order.

70. From the viewpoint of the relationship between law and custom as independent normative sources used for establishing Constitutional systems, three distinct modalities are usually found:

(1) *constitutional systems that are essentially customary*: they assign the most relevance to Constitutional custom, pushing the Constitutional Law and jurisprudence into a secondary position, as is the case in the United Kingdom;
(2) *semi-customary systems*: they confer equal relevance to the law and to Constitutional custom, as in the case of the Third French Republic; and
(3) *subsidiarily customary Constitutional systems*: which accept the relevance of Constitutional custom only at a secondary level, as is the case of the American Constitutional system.

71. This classification, however, is far from exhaustive:

- the first modality cannot exist as such because every Constitutional system always needs to be supported by legal rules and their simple presence hinders the qualification of the system as essentially customary; and
- the second and third modalities are, on the contrary, the most probable hypotheses, for it is a general characteristic of theirs to confer only a limited relevance upon Constitutional custom *vis-à-vis* Constitutional Law.

It should be stressed here that Constitutional custom could never stand on its own in view of the fact that, in contemporary states, this branch of the law consists mandatorily of norms and principles with a different origin – a legal origin, that is to say that they stem from a voluntary act named the Constitution.

Consequently the issue of the relevance of the so-called Customary Constitutional Law should not be considered on its own since this topic is being examined within the framework of other norms and principles, which, jointly, build up that branch of the law.

There is no doubt that in theoretical terms it is possible to conceive a strictly customary Constitutional system. In our technological world, however, where social and political relations are increasingly complex, such a system would not be feasible.

This is why we must always opt for the diminished relevance of Constitutional custom and never its absolute or indeed essential relevance.

72. More important than the hypotheses of a relationship between custom and law as systematic sources that share the same normative space is the question of the legitimacy of custom's role in the framing of the Constitutional order, within the Constitution versus Constitutional custom.

Traditionally, there may be considered to be three types of relationship between custom and law, the same scheme applying to the relations between the Constitution and Constitutional custom:

- *secundum legem* custom, *which follows the voluntarily enacted Constitutional norms and principles*;
- *praeter legem* custom, *which goes further than the voluntarily enacted norms and principles*; and
- *contra legem* custom, *which proves contrary to the voluntarily enacted norms and principles.*

We must assume that each of these modalities may be relevant within the framework of Constitutional Law.

With regard to the first two categories, they seem quite natural in view of the fact that Constitutional circumstances are equally sensitive to the effects of coexistence that may be produced by customary norms, either in the community of citizens or within Constitutional institutions.

The acceptability of the *contra-constitutionem* custom, however, is more debatable. It is clear that there is not the intention to jeopardize an entire Constitutional system built as a result of intentional Constitution-making acts, on the basis of a legal will to erect it.

The real issue is whether to accept the production by custom of norms and principles that may, in some cases, reject Constitutional norms and principles of a legal nature.

73. The usual arguments put forward in the circumstances tend towards favouring the non-acceptance of *contra-constitutionem* custom based, apart from the structural hostility of the Constitution to the informality of customary expressions, on three lines of reasoning:

(1) that, on the one hand, customary norms could never rule against the provisions of the Constitution. The latter would only validate them if it accepted them; but then, the general question of *contra legem* would disappear;

(2) that, on the other hand, customary norms were formed with disregard to the procedures for Constitutional amendment, thus appearing as a marginal power, expressing itself 'savagely' outside the Constitutional framework; and
(3) finally, that customary norms were formed in breach of the Constitution-making will, a very serious circumstance, the more so when considering that the latter, when comparing the general democratic legitimacy of the Constitutional text with the very limited popular legitimacy of a Constitutional provision eventually produced by custom and rejecting that will, would be found to be progressively more democratic.

The fact, however, is that the above arguments do not seem to apply in every circumstance and, therefore, the legitimacy of custom as an autonomous source of Constitutional Law should be admitted, emphasizing, nevertheless, at the same time, that, in practice, its role is limited as a result of the technological world in which we live.

74. The first argument, according to which *contra-constitutionem* custom cannot have significance because it has to be authorized by the Constitution as an intentional and legal source, should be discarded at once. It is obvious that this modality, due to its nature, should be placed at the heart of a conflict between the customary approach on one side and the legal one on the other. The legitimacy of custom, if taken in its most profound and genuine sense, is found in custom itself and, as such, in order to exist, does not have to ask the law for permission.

Neither are the other two arguments admissible since they originate in a mistaken presupposition: that the nature of constituent power is exclusively legal and that, once it has been expressed, its realization is only possible within the exact terms of its initial manifestation, that is, the Constitution as adopted.

Constitution-making power is not a static power or a power that can only irrupt from time to time: it exists at all times and can also take the form of customary norms as long as that is what the interested political community wants in terms of self-regulation. It goes without saying that the procedure of Constitutional reform only makes sense when aimed at framing a legal power, but certainly not with regard to a manifestation of a juridical character such as customary norms.

From another standpoint and in what concerns the principle of democracy – although this is not the only Constitutional principle – the expression of customary norms also reflects the above principle, albeit to a much lesser degree. Somewhat ironically, it is possible to say that this is the most democratic and accepted of all powers in view of the obligatory coincidence between being and having to be that custom, by its own nature, postulates.

§2. Practical Limitation of Constitutional Jurisprudence

75. Another normative source to consider in Constitutional Law is *Constitutional jurisprudence*, which implies the production of legal rules and principles by way of the activity of the judiciary in connection with the application of the Constitution.

This is not a dimension frequently found in jurisprudence in general, since it consists in the application of the law to concrete cases according to the organizing perspective, which distinguishes the judiciary, and with the inherent characteristics of independence, impartiality and responsibility.

Sometimes, however, jurisprudence decrees the general validity of certain guidelines based on the everyday vicissitudes of applying the legal precepts and it establishes, in that way, certain interpretations that take on a normative character.

And when that occurs in Constitutional Law we must regard jurisprudence as a source of that law. Such cases, however, are rare. Consequently, this is always a secondary source and the cases at issue must be specifically framed within positive Constitutional Law.

76. The search for the value of jurisprudence as a source of Constitutional Law should be accompanied by a parallel concern for finding normative solutions within this branch of the law in accordance with the jurisdictional bodies that are entitled to apply it.

Few doubts seem to arise concerning the pertinence of the various jurisdictional bodies when it comes to the application of Constitutional Law. The concept of this law has long, left behind any notion of being an internal branch dedicated to organization in favour of a material concept, which fully irradiates unto the farthest corners of the legal order.

Nowadays all powers are bound to the Constitution – therefore, judicial power is equally bound to it – and, consequently, there are no vacua of immunity or of non-application of the Constitution.

The normative significance of jurisprudence in connection with Constitutional Law shall derive from the terms under which the action of the courts, as bodies entrusted with the enforcement of the sources of law, is generically provided for. This ensues from the fact that the parameters relating to the juridical system by which they must abide do not exclude Constitutional Law, since the courts can also accede to the Constitution as a parameter for the application of the law in the cases they are called upon to judge.

77. The above apparently far-reaching conclusion must, nevertheless, be corrected in view of the fact that certain jurisdictional bodies – such as the Constitutional Court in Portugal – are vested with a specific role in dealing with Constitutional issues.

Its role in the application of Constitutional Law is not exclusive; nevertheless, it will end up by being exclusivist when you consider the particular form the power of the Constitutional Court takes when issuing decisions that shall be regarded as sources of Constitutional Law.

In what circumstances does it happen? It may happen in the exact circumstances under which jurisprudence assumes the normative role specifically vested in it: that is, when it declares a generally binding unconstitutionality.

However, even under these circumstances, it may be difficult to grasp why the intervention of the Constitutional Court is primarily negative given that the *erga omnes* binding effect only concerns its rulings of unconstitutionality.

It is undeniable that a big effort is needed if we are to deduce a positive normative guidance from such rulings, a 'must be' intended to impose compliance with a Constitutional rule or principle and not with some sub-Constitutional source.

78. Apart from the above-mentioned cases, the significance of Constitutional jurisprudence – issued by all the courts but in particular by the Constitutional Court

– can only be regarded as normative. It cannot be said to represent either truly or formally a source of Constitutional Law.

On the contrary, the application of Constitutional Law is only binding on the case under trial. The foregoing does not imply that it is not important, nowadays more than ever, to study and examine the rulings of the Constitutional Court, as well as those of the other courts (albeit less relevant), for many reasons, the least of which is not that they have been entrusted with the task of filling in, through their intervention within the margin left to sub-Constitutional power, many spaces the Constitution has not occupied.

Nevertheless a distinction should obviously be drawn between planes: it is one thing to say that when the courts enforce Constitutional Law it is useful to be aware of their judgments, so that each and every citizen may anticipate how they will rule in the future; another, radically different thing, is to view their decisions when enforcing Constitutional Law as mandatory and to feel compelled in the future – in particular in the case of the judges – to follow a previous interpretation or application of a rule in light of the Constitution because that would make no sense, not even if a provision for precedents might exist.

§3. Exclusion of Other Sources of Constitutional Law

79. The traditional list of sources of law, hereunder the specific perspective of Constitutional Law, is not yet complete, but the essential points have been dealt with.

It remains to be explained why other alleged sources of law in general, under their specific role as putative sources of Constitutional Law, have been dismissed. To these should also be added the Constitutional conventions that do not belong in the general list.

These sources are:

- *constitutional doctrine*;
- *general constitutional principles*;
- *constitutional equity*; and
- *constitutional conventions*.

80. Doctrine in the field of law – within this possible meaning, which is not to be confused with political, ideological or religious doctrines – represents the opinion of the jurists and academics on the applicable sources. Often results that are quite useful for identifying the sources stem from doctrine, in particular when the jurists or the professors are the material authors of normative acts.

However, it does not flow from the above that nowadays *Constitutional doctrine* is relevant as a source of Constitutional Law since the opinion of academics does not seem to be binding on the interpretation of the Constitutional norms and principles, although it is thanks to their expression, and the usually ensuing discussion, that highly satisfactory solutions can be reached.

The predominant understanding has not always been the foregoing and it should be noted that, in the past, alongside the traditionally acknowledged legal sources, the opinion of certain jurists, regarded as true 'lawmakers', was highly esteemed.

Yet this conclusion could never impose itself in Constitutional Law for a variety of reasons, and for an additional one closely connected with its inherent political dimension: its proximity to the political debate, by inhibiting, most of the time, neutral doctrinarian positions, makes it harder for Constitutional doctrine to be able to contribute, as a normative source, to this legal branch.

81. Another situation sometimes quoted as a source of law in general, which can, consequently, be equally of interest to Constitutional Law, is that of the general principles of law.

It is not deserving of any particular comment within the framework of Constitutional Law since everything that has been previously said, in general, about it also applies here: *the general principles of Constitutional Law* are, by themselves, a very important part of Constitutional Law rather than sources of Constitutional Law.

How could anything be simultaneously 'the thing in itself and the source from which it springs'? This would be an enormous legal and logical nonsense since general Constitutional principles, together with Constitutional laws and provisions, are component parts of the legal order.

82. Equity is the last secondary source of law in general to be mentioned in this context of exclusion from the sources of Constitutional Law, notwithstanding the fact that it is admitted as a hypothetic source of law in general. We should keep in mind what the Civil Code asserts with respect to it.

Constitutional Law, namely the CRP, also alludes to it when stating that the Constitutional Court, in given circumstances, might decide based on equity: 'When legal security, reasons of equity or public interest of exceptional importance, which have to be justified, requires it, the Constitutional Court may fix the effects of unconstitutionality or illegality in a more restrictive way than is provided for in paragraphs (1) and (2)' (Article 282(4) of the CRP).

This constitutes an exceptional device that permits the emergence of other reasons, which defeat the reasons imposed by the principle of constitutionality and lead to the incomplete invalidation of unconstitutional acts of public law, as could be normally expected of the application of that principle taken in its adjective form of perfect law.

Nevertheless with regard to the present possibility, together with other reasons invoked, the truth is that it cannot really be identified as a source of Constitutional Law. What occurs in the event is not the supremacy of the Constitution but rather the predominance of a reason of equity, which, in the given circumstance, allows the equity of a concrete case to be pondered.

83. Constitutional conventions, as apparently specific Constitutional sources, presuppose that political agreements with regard to certain given aspects of the operation of the political system have been reached, similar to those achieved in other areas – they are very frequent in international political activity or in the world of business – and called gentlemen's agreements.

However, these Constitutional conventions do not assume any of the features of the Constitutional provisions; they are meant to remain on the outside of the

Constitutional sphere, as attested by the fact that there are no provisions in the event of their infringement.

Even their authors, in spite of intending to invest them with normative power, never ponder the possibility of calling on the judicial system in order to obtain their coercive enforcement.

Chapter 4. The Non-constitutional Sources of Portuguese Law

§1. General Framework of the Public Law Functions and Acts and Their Hierarchy

84. The organization of public power comprises necessarily the public law acts that give practical effect to the will of the State institutions, which, in this way, acquire legal relevance.

The public law acts are the concrete expression of the public law functions, the latter being the name denoting the activities of the public bodies within a range with much broader characteristics. And one and the same legal function finds expression in a variety of acts.

But, when defining each function, instead of separating them from the connected diverse modalities of acts, it seems more to the point to consider them jointly.

85. As the evolution of the Constitutional State has shown, both the public law functions and the corresponding public law acts present, nowadays, quite a different picture from the one idealized by John Locke and Charles De Montesquieu and put into practice shortly later, in the Constitutional texts of the nineteenth century.

The changes that occurred at the turn of the nineteenth to the twentieth century had many different causes that led to the multiplication of the public law functions and a general easing of the formerly rigid divides between them.

Despite those changes, however, the corrected functional divide is still valid. The four different criteria for distinguishing them from one another are:

(1) *the material criterion*, that considers the contents, as well as the scopes to be attained by their exercise;
(2) *the formal criterion*, that considers the mode of formation and procedure followed;
(3) *the organic criterion*, that considers the respective organ and the mode of appointment of its members; and
(4) *the hierarchical criterion*, that considers the position occupied in the gradation of the legal order.

86. In our view, the description of the public law functions and acts fits into the following table that presents them in hierarchical order:

- the Constitutional function and Constitutional acts (mentioned above);
- the international function and international conventions;
- the legislative function and legislative acts;
- the political function and political acts;
- the administrative function and administrative acts; and
- the judicial function and judicial acts.

§2. INTERNATIONAL FUNCTION AND INTERNATIONAL CONVENTIONS

87. From the perspective of Portuguese Constitutional Law, the rules of procedure applicable to the drafting of international conventions, if rightly read, provide for the previously mentioned *summa divisio* between solemn treaties and simplified agreements (executive-agreements), two species of the class 'international convention or treaty' in the broader sense.

This is a case where, behind a difference in terminology, considerable differences in the rules of procedure have developed. It is, therefore, advisable to describe separately some of the phases of their conclusion at the domestic level.

Among the differences, the following are worthy of note:

- *in the phase of approval*, solemn treaties always fall within the competence of Parliament (*Assembleia da República*), whereas agreements may be approved either by it or by the government;
- *in the phase of binding*, the ratification of solemn treaties expresses the will of the Portuguese State to be bound by them, whereas in the case of simplified agreements only approval by Parliament or the government is required; and
- *in the case of preventive review*, solemn treaties can be confirmed after having been declared unconstitutional, whereas the same does not apply to simplified agreements, at least following a literal interpretation of the law.

88. Portuguese law does not provide for the conclusion of agreements in the form of an exchange of notes/letters since that would eliminate the intervention of the Head of State and thus exclude from the process such a fundamental organ of our political system.

The drafting of international conventions consists of five phases:

(1) negotiation;
(2) adoption of the text;
(3) domestic approval;
(4) conferment of binding force; and
(5) publication and enforcement.

89. The first and second stages in the international perspective – *the negotiation and adoption of the document* – are jointly dealt with at the national level in the so-called phase of 'negotiation and adjustment' of international conventions.

In light of the CRP's text, that power is entrusted to the Government, within the scope of the exercise of its political function, and it is akin to international relations: 'The Government, in the exercise of political functions has the power to negotiate and adjust international conventions' (Article 197(1)(b) of the CRP).

90. The third stage of *domestic approval* does not find a direct correspondence at the international law level, but it is an important moment for the politico-democratic legitimacy of the international conventions in question.

Curiously, this stage usually has no international effects, which proves the point that it is a result of the diversification of the forms of representation in the political systems established after the emergence of Constitutionalism.

However, it cannot be overlooked since it has considerable implications for increasing the popular legitimacy of international treaties – a praiseworthy intent.

The distinction between treaties and agreements must be clearly drawn in these circumstances.

In what concerns *solemn treaties*, the power for their approval lies always with Parliament, irrespective of the subject matter. This competence is reserved to Parliament.

With regard to *simplified agreements*, the power of approval varies:

- either it rests with *Parliament* whenever the subject matters of the international convention are, by analogy, comprised in the sphere reserved to the legislative power of Parliament; or, notwithstanding the fact that it normally holds that power, the Government chooses to bestow it on Parliament, thereby achieving broader politico-democratic legitimacy; and
- or it rests with *the Government* whenever the two possibilities already referred in the preceding paragraph do not occur: in this context, the Government's primary power to approve simplified agreements whenever they do not deal with matters reserved to the legislative power of Parliament should be pointed out.

91. The fourth stage, that is the consent to be bound to the contents of international conventions, also follows a different procedure depending on whether the convention is a solemn treaty or a simplified agreement.

Solemn treaties, according to the custom and rules of international law, require the intervention of the Head of State, who signs a letter of ratification and, at the domestic level, a presidential decree of ratification.

Simplified agreements, because they are simplified, do without an autonomous phase of consent to be bound, thus having the advantage of joining, in one and the same moment – the act of signature, the adoption of the text and the consent to be bound by it, whereas in the case of solemn treaties there are two different moments.

92. From the viewpoint of Portuguese law, the fifth and last stage to be mentioned is that of *the publication and coming into force of the international conventions*, to which Portugal has become a party.

The place it takes at the end of the domestic process by which conventions are concluded is self-evident since, once the content of their text has been fixed and the remaining procedural acts carried out, all that remains is to give notice of them to the community at large.

Only after that notice can they come into force in accordance with the rule of law, this being entirely reversed at the international level where conventions first come into force and are subsequently registered and published.

The publication of international conventions in Portuguese law is a generically mentioned condition assigned to a moment preceding its entry into force. Publication of the convention in the official journal (*Diário da República*) is a condition of its efficacy under the provision that deals with the incorporation of international law in Portuguese law. The latter only admits the coming into force after publication: 'The provisions of international conventions duly ratified or adopted come into force in the domestic legal order after their official publication and remain so as long as they are binding on Portugal' (Article 8(2) of the CRP).

§3. Legislative Function and Legislative Acts

93. The legislative function, despite not being the supreme public law function, is probably the most consolidated of them all, reflecting the daily concern with the structure of the State and society.

The legislative function has usually had a normative character and deals with the definition of public/general interest by democratic political organs in a direct or an indirect way.

The move towards the social and the post-social State has changed this characteristic and nowadays we are frequently faced with legislative acts that are not normative in content.

94. The expression of the legislative function in legislative acts takes the form of law. In the CRP it may assume four distinct forms:

(1) *organic laws (leis orgânicas)*, within the powers of Parliament. These are legislative acts that deal with the more sensitive matters and in doing so reflect the particular supremacy of Parliament (Article 166(2) of the CRP);
(2) *acts (leis)*, within the powers of Parliament. They appear as a residual category within the legislative function of the national Parliament (Article 166(3) of the CRP);
(3) *decree-laws (decretos-leis)*, within the powers of the executive. They manifest themselves in the areas that are not reserved to Parliament and to the autonomous regions. Furthermore, there are areas exclusively reserved to the legislative function of the executive, such as the matters of its own organization and operation (Article 198 of the CRP); and
(4) *regional legislative decrees (decretos legislativos regionais)*, within the power of the legislative assemblies of the autonomous regions. They deal with the range of matters in relation to which these regional bodies have the power to enact legislation (Article 227 of the CRP).

§4. Political Function and Political Acts

95. The *political function* denotes, in a residual way, the public law activities involved in the definition of public/general interest, whenever that purpose cannot be served by any other existing function or act in the realm of public law.

From the material perspective, the political function is associated with the definition of general interest entrusted primarily to the main organs of government possessing democratic legitimacy but, at the same time, the legislative act form is rejected.

The political function does not belong within the fundamental doctrinal core of the separation of powers; it was subsequently added, but has been advancing in various directions. Among its many concerns, the control of public power stands out.

96. The political function expresses itself through the existence of a wide range of *political acts*:

- *electoral acts*: elections express the will of the electoral body to designate persons to hold offices, which have been submitted to the popular vote, this being a case where the people are the authors of a public law act (Article 119(1)(i) of the CRP);
- *acts of a referendum nature*: referendums also express the will of the citizens; in the circumstances, with regard to issues that are submitted to their binding decision (Articles 115 and 240 of the CRP); and
- *acts of a governing nature*: a multitude of acts that have to do with impelling and vitalizing the system of government, such as parliamentary motions, the acts of appointment, removal from office and dissolution, as well as normative acts that do not take the legislative form (Article 166(4)(5) of the CRP).

§5. Administrative Function and Administrative Acts

97. The *administrative function* is a public activity of a secondary nature related to the satisfaction of the collective needs of the State/society.

It operates at a second level of the definition of public interest and is exercised by administrative bodies, which are not, as a general rule, democratically legitimized.

However, this function has the undeniable advantage of a closer proximity to the citizens, who see, through it, their collective needs being satisfied and problems being solved, the solution of which is the government's responsibility.

98. The *administrative function* materializes itself in the production of administrative acts, such as, for instance:

- *administrative rules and regulations (regulamentos administrativos)*: they represent the will to provide a normative order of a permanent or general character in relation to the organization and operation of administrative institutions, or to a particular area of the activities of those under their administration (Article 112(6)(7) of the CRP);
- *administrative acts*: concrete and individual decisions taken by the public administration in pursuance of the law and of administrative rules and regulations and which establish the legal situation of citizens under that administration;
- *administrative contracts*: agreements of will between two or more parties, that formulate and articulate the rights and duties of the contractors in the prosecution of public interest as laid down within the framework of public administration.

§6. Judicial Function and Judicial Acts

99. The *judicial function* completes the range of public law functions. It refers to the application of law previously enacted by independent and impartial organs and its scope is to determine the disputes submitted to them.

The judicial function is not in every case the responsibility of the judiciary as already hinted by the existing possibility that arbitral courts may act as judicial bodies despite not belonging to the public judicial function.

It should be added that the performance of the judicial function is not merely applicative and non-normative; sometimes there may be cases of judicial creation and normativity.

100. Judicial acts can assume many different forms, according to the range of possibilities that the exercise of the judicial function offers:

- *final decisions and interlocutory decisions (decisões finais, despachos interlocutórios)*: final decisions when they put an end to a dispute before a given court and interlocutory decisions when they are made in the course of the procedure;
- *judgments (sentenças e acórdãos judiciais)*: the first are the final decisions made by a single judge, while the latter are the final decisions of collective courts, where several judges sit on the bench.

Chapter 5. Legislative Function, Legislative Acts and in Particular Legislative Procedure

§1. Definition of the Legislative Function

101. When examining the exercise of public power by the State and the other bodies that may eventually share the same function, the *legislative function* stands out on account of its relevance. It can be defined according to four approaches:

(1) *the subject matter approach*, the legislative function expresses the definition of the major choices made by the community and the State in their search for the wider public interest;
(2) *the formal approach*, the legislative function is exercised with full freedom of choice and respect for its inherent distinctive features of pluralism and duty of publication;
(3) *the organic approach*, the legislative function depends directly on the people for its democratic legitimacy; and
(4) *the hierarchical approach*, the legislative function is located immediately below the Constitutional function as it expresses the conjunctional organization of society.

102. Conscious of the relevance of the legislative function and acts, the CRP set out some important principles in connection with the lawmaking process, three of which should be underlined here: the principle of competence, the principle of typification and the principle of functional binding force.

Under the *competence principle* the organs, which are, at a given time, empowered to enact legislation cannot simply, of their own will, or by way of a delegation mechanism, cease to be empowered. The changes in competences have to be provided for under the Constitution and alterations to the competences are not allowed outside of these conditions.

Under the *principle of typification*, relating to the forms of the law, it is required that legal force be conferred solely on those acts, which are declared as such by the Constitution. No other act can pretend, for itself or for another act, to have a different legal effect from the one assigned by the CRP to that type of public law act.

The *principle of the functional binding force* implies that, regardless of their equal hierarchical standing, some legislative acts can prevail over others by reason of the particular function they perform, and cannot be repealed unless the act under which they are repealed takes their place in respect of the same organizing function.

§2. Reserved Matters and Lawmaking Competence

103. The existence of *matters reserved to the lawmaking power (reserva de lei)* implies that the legislative acts are specifically located in the various places they may occupy within the range of existing public law acts.

The enshrinement of the exclusivity of lawmaking power with regard to certain reserved matters inhibits the enactment of any other type of public law acts in the same respect. If a given matter falls under the exclusive competence of the lawmaking bodies, no room is left for the intervention of any other public law act.

Consequently, the fact that a given matter falls within matters reserved to the exclusive legislative competence abolishes the possibility that it might be dealt with, for a normative purpose, by other normative bodies, within other public law functions.

In this context, the most noteworthy aspect is the relationship with the acts produced by the administrative function, namely, administrative rules and regulations.

104. Reserved matters can exist in relation to all the specific legislative acts established by the Constitutional system. The higher the variety of acts, the more important it becomes to make a clear distinction between them since reserved matters, should there be a variety of acts, shall be reserved to certain laws or to certain legislative acts.

It follows that we are faced with a number of possible modalities according to the operative criteria used to establish the more meaningful contrapositions encountered in this context:

- matters reserved to the Constitution and matters reserved to the law;
- matters exclusively reserved or matters partially reserved;
- matters reserved to national law and matters reserved to regional law; and
- matters reserved to parliamentary law and matters reserved to government legislation.

105. We should now examine the terms under which *legislative competence* has been conferred by the CRP within the overall assignment of functions to the various organs of government as laid down by this document. It has already been made clear that legislative acts do not originate in one sole entity and even less in a unique organ of a public law nature.

Legislative competence denotes the capacity of the public bodies to produce legislative acts by virtue of the legislative function they are called upon to share.

106. Different approaches enable us to identify the different modalities of legislative competence, such as those laid down in Portuguese Constitutional Law:

- *the criterion of the collective body* to which it belongs: legislative competence of the State and legislative competence of a non-State body, such as the autonomous regions;
- *the criterion of the organ of government* on which it is vested: legislative competence of Parliament and legislative competence of the government, depending on whether the organ in question is Parliament or the government; if it is Parliament, it can be the national Parliament or a regional Parliament;

- *the criterion of exclusive empowerment or joint empowerment*: exclusive legislative competence, delegated legislative competence, joint legislative competence, depending on whether only its holder exercises it, the holder can, by his/her own decision, allow another organ to exercise it, or the holder coexists with one or more other organ;
- *the criterion of the Constitutional definition* relating to the organ empowered with it: generic legislative competence, specific legislative competence and residual legislative competence, depending on whether the competence is defined in terms of general concepts, or of certain specified types of matters or conferred on the grounds that a given matter is not, from that perspective, within the power of any other organ;
- *the criterion of the intensity of its expression*: full legislative competence, general legislative competence, main legislative competence and framing legislative competence depending on whether it comprises the entirety of the subject matter, or is meant for the provision of general rules, or concerns solely the laying down of basic principles to be developed in further legislation, or respects the production of framework laws; and
- *the criterion of the circumstances of enactment*: ordinary legislative competence and extraordinary legislative competence, depending on whether the competence is exercised in the course of the public law ordinary activities of the legislative bodies, or in the extraordinary circumstances of an urgent procedure.

107. It becomes easier to understand the distribution of legislative competence, resulting in the subsequent enactment of various legislative acts under the above-mentioned classifying criteria, if we resort to the types of legislative competence provided in Portuguese Constitutional Law on the basis of the organs that are vested with the competence:

- distribution along a horizontal line; and
- distribution along a vertical line.

Horizontally, the distribution of power occurs within each collective body that has legislative power. Various possibilities arise here with regard to the distribution of duties within the scope of lawmaking.

Vertically, it occurs within the relationship between the State and other collective bodies empowered with legislative competence, such as, in the case of Portugal, the autonomous regions, by way of their legislative assemblies.

108. The CRP makes a horizontal distribution within the State when it vests legislative competence – that is the power to produce legislative acts – in two of the organs of government: Parliament and the Government.

As a result of the sharing of the legislative function by these two organs, four different categories of *legislative power* can be identified:

(1) *exclusive legislative power of Parliament*: the entire range of matters reserved to Parliament, on which Parliament alone is entitled to legislate. They comprise the

essential core of laws as a tribute paid to the political and legislative relevance of that institution;

(2) *legislative power that can be delegated by Parliament*: the entire range of matters, on which Parliament can either itself legislate or choose to delegate the power to the Government by way of a legislative authorization;

(3) *legislative power of the government*: the entire range of matters, on which the Government alone is empowered to legislate; the possibility of delegating said power to another institution is not admissible, not even to Parliament; and

(4) *joint legislative power*: the entire range of matters, by far the most extensive of them all, on which both Parliament and the Government are empowered to legislate freely, thus producing acts that may amend or repeal one another.

109. Let us now consider the vertical perspective in the distribution of legislative competence. In this case the relationship is between the State and the autonomous regions and there are subject matters that fall within the legislative power of either one or the other. Understandably, the most important subject matters fall within the power of the Republic rather than within that of the autonomous regions.

Yet this does not mean that, in a regionalized and relatively decentralized State such as the Portuguese, there are not important matters about which the autonomous regions hold legislative power. The legislative power of the autonomous regions can be described as follows:

- *primary regional legislative power*: the power to adopt regional legislative decrees within the scope of their legislative autonomy;
- *authorized regional legislative power*: the power to approve regional legislative decrees concerning subject matters, which, on account of falling within the matters partly reserved to the legislative power of Parliament, require the latter's authorization; and
- *regional legislative power for developing other legislation*: the power to pass decrees, which confer density on the laws that lay down the basic principles and guidance regarding a given issue, provided that the regional legislative assemblies are not inhibited from carrying out said development.

§3. The Types of Legislative Acts

110. For various reasons connected not only with a preoccupation with the division of the legislative function between Parliament and the Government, but also with the existence of autonomous regions with legislative functions, legislative acts in Portugal are of four types, the first three being enacted by the State and the fourth type by the autonomous regions:

(1) *Organic Laws of Parliament*;
(2) *Laws (stricto sensu) or Acts of Parliament*;
(3) *Decree-Laws of the Government*; and

(4) *Regional Legislative Decrees enacted by the legislative assemblies of the autonomous regions.*

111. The *Acts of Parliament*, in contrast to what might be expected, are nowadays extremely complex; hence, it is not entirely appropriate to state that there is one law of Parliament, when in truth there are many laws of Parliament, depending on their organizing function, procedural requirements or formal qualification:

- *depending on their form*: organic laws and acts (Constitutional laws do not belong here, they fall within the scope of the Constitutional function and acts);
- *depending on the intensity of lawmaking*: laws laying down basic principles and guidelines, laws enabling the government and the legislative assemblies of the autonomous regions to pass laws, framework laws and laws.

Reinforced laws take on a particular prevailing force over other laws, partly on specific grounds stemming from the provisions under which they are enacted or due to their subordinating force with regard to other legislative acts.

112. The national government's legislative acts take the form of so-called decree-laws and must be approved by the Council of Ministers, which is the most extensive acting structure of the government in its collective dimension.

The Government is entitled to take four types of legislative acts within one single category of acts according to the above-mentioned classification. In contrast to Parliament and the regional assemblies, in this case there is no relation with the legislative function of the autonomous regions.

The four types are the following:

(1) *exclusive 'decree-laws'*: 'The Government has exclusive competence in matters concerning its own organization and working' (Article 198(2) of the CRP);
(2) *concurring 'decree-laws'*: 'decree-laws on matters not reserved to the Assembly of the Republic' (Article 198(1)(a) of the CRP);
(3) *authorized 'decree-laws'*: 'decree-laws on matters relatively reserved to the Assembly of the Republic subject to its authorization' (Article 198(1)(b) of the CRP); and
(4) *implementation 'decree-laws'*: 'decree-laws pursuant to laws laying down basic principles and guidelines *(leis de bases)*' (Article 198(1)(c) of the CRP).

113. The power of enactment of the legislative acts of the autonomous regions rests always with the respective legislative assemblies, notwithstanding the existence of other bodies in the Regional Government system, such as, for instance, the regional governments, which do not share the regional legislative power.

The regional legislative decrees – this is the name given to regional legislative acts – worthy of note are the following:

- *exclusive regional legislative decrees*: enacted under primary regional legislative competence;

- *authorized regional legislative decrees*: enacted under regional legislative competence authorized by the Republic; and
- *regional legislative decrees of implementation*: enacted under the regional legislative competence to implement the basic principles of legal regimes.

§4. The Organic Laws in Particular

114. Among the variety of legislative acts, the category of *organic law* assumes a special place. Created by virtue of the fourth Constitutional reform, they now constitute an autonomous type of legislative act, separately numbered in the official journal (*Diário da República*).

This novel category of legislative acts can only be rightly understood if one bears in mind the background of its Constitutional embodiment that dates back to a Constitutional reform bill intended to enshrine so-called para-constitutional laws requiring, like Constitutional amendments, a qualified majority of two-thirds of the members present or represented.

Since that notion, in those exact terms, did not gain approval, agreement was reached on the enactment of a surrogate, less demanding on the parliamentary will: the organic laws.

115. The logical consistency of the introduction of organic law arises from the notion that there are matters, which on the grounds of their relevance must be subject, in order to be enacted, to more demanding legal rules in terms of those willing to advance them.

It is, however, debatable whether the final outcome coincides with the initial motivation. Granted that such a coincidence exists with regard to the choice of the matters and to the specific conditions of the vote, it remains questionable whether simply moving from relative to absolute majority make the expression of the will more encompassing.

Should any doubts remain about the interest, from a legal and political viewpoint, of the organic laws, it would suffice to watch the Portuguese political and parliamentary practice over the last years to notice that little or nothing has changed after the creation of the said category in terms of an effective valorization of parliamentary activity.

116. On the contrary, it should be acknowledged that, despite a late and difficult birth, the Constitutional design of the organic laws laudably respects the need for a minimum of clarity. Consequently, and taking as reference the parameters of the law of Parliament, as well as the parliamentary lawmaking procedure, the following specificities can be observed:

- *on the subjective level*, similar to laws, organic laws fall within the exclusive power of Parliament and cannot be enacted by the Government or by the regional assemblies (Article 162(2) of the CRP);
- *on the material level*, organic laws, immediately after the Constitutional amendment acts, deal with the most relevant legislative subject matters (*see* the subject matters detailed in (a) to (f), (h), (j), the first part of paragraph (l) (q) and (t) of Article 164 and Article 255 of the CRP);

- *on the procedural level*, organic laws must be passed, at the final global vote, by a qualified two-thirds majority of the deputies where that majority exceeds an absolute majority of the deputies entitled to vote (Article 168(5) of the CRP);
- *on the formal level*, organic laws receive their own private legislative form and are, as a result, numbered separately; and
- *on the level of guarantees*, the active procedural legitimacy of the power of initiative with regard to anticipatory Constitutional review of organic laws is considerably extended to comprise also the prime minister and one-fifth of the members of Parliament (Article 278(4) of the CRP).

§5. The Lawmaking Process

117. If we are to obtain a better insight into the enactment of parliamentary legislative acts, which is our main concern, we should examine each of the stages of the process where it is possible to identify some specific effect that contributes to the final legislative act.

The procedural stages are as follows:

- *the stage of initiation*;
- *the stage of scrutiny and amendment*;
- *the stage of decision*; and
- *the stage of efficacy.*

118. The stage of legislative initiation – which we may also simply call legislative initiation – is the moment when the making of a legislative act begins its journey.

This power to launch the legislative process should not be confused with the power to decide on the legislative act itself, or to pass it. The relevant functional powers do not have to be wielded by one and the same entity: it is not mandatory that the powers of initiative lie with the organ that has the power to pass legislation and vice versa.

The power to initiate the legislative process is not uniform; it admits various combinations:

- *internal initiative and external initiative*, depending on whether the process starts within Parliament – with the deputies, parliamentary political groups or specialized committees (or, eventually, other bodies), or outside Parliament – with the government, the other parliamentary bodies, such as the legislative assemblies of the autonomous regions or even with citizens (the popular or citizens initiative);
- *general initiative and specific initiative* according to the breadth of the power to initiate at issue, the first being the power to initiate a legislative process relative to all and every issue and the second a power to be exercised only in regard to certain given issues, more limited than the former;
- *reserved initiative and concurring initiative* depending on whether the power of initiative is exclusively held by a given body or, on the contrary, whether there

is the possibility that more than one body holds that power in respect of certain given matters; and

- *original initiative and supervening initiative* based on whether the power of initiative is exercised at an initial moment or, on the contrary, after other bodies have already exercised their own power of legislative initiative, taking in the latter case the form of an amendment, a replacement, an addition or a revocation.

119. The stage of legislative scrutiny and modification represents a second moment of reflection over the meaning of the draft legislation, following the first expression of will that occurs at the stage of legislative initiative, and it may be convenient and sometimes even necessary, at this stage, to obtain additional information and opinions in order to produce better laws:

- *convenient* because it may be useful to call on more opinions and the expertise of people who are technically qualified with regard to the topics at issue; and
- *necessary* because, due to the sensitivity of certain fields, it is justified to make it mandatory to seek the advice and comment of affected people and organizations in an open and combined approach to the formation of legislative acts.

This inquiry is carried out by the relevant general committee (*comissão especializada*), which is usually a standing committee, although it is also possible to set up an ad hoc committee 'where the relevance and specialization of the issue so justifies'.

120. The stage of legislative decision comprises the most significant moment of the entire process, where the climax in the expression of the will to make law is reached.

This stage, the constitutive moment of the lawmaking process, divides itself into several sub-moments, as a result of the conjunction of wills of the various intervening bodies required at this point:

- *the approval by Parliament*, by way of a first reading generic vote, a second reading vote on details and, finally, an overall final vote;
- *the promulgation by the President of the Republic*, an act that is equally necessary for the act to exist in law; and
- *the prime minister's counter-signature*, on the presidential decree of promulgation, on behalf of the government.

The decision stage of the national legislative process is assuredly, notwithstanding the somewhat pared-down description of its various moments that has been given here, the most substantial stage, encapsulating the moment of decision, on which the decision to make the law rests.

One should, however, dissociate an internal constitutive moment – which occurs within the walls of the Parliament – and an external constitutive moment – which occurs beyond Parliament and requires the intervention of other bodies.

The decision by Parliament is at the heart of that constitutive moment and it comprises the approval of the law after it has gone through the stages of initiative, scrutiny and inquiry.

The other moment that occurs at the constitutive stage of the national legislative process links the final will of the parliamentary institution to the intervention of other external bodies, which are empowered to act in this respect by the Constitution.

121. The stage of legislative efficacy corresponds to the entry into force of the law and it requires the implementation of a number of appropriate procedures.

To comply with the demands of the rule of law, it is necessary that the law be conveniently publicized so that the prescription of normative rules acquires transparency and secret legal rules are banned.

This is the only way in which the political community at large may get to know the law that rules it, thereby avoiding the existence of hidden sources.

The publication of all laws in the official State journal – the *Diário da República*, which promotes the dissemination of their contents – formally fulfils this requirement.

It goes without saying that the publication in the official journal does not preclude the use of other means of publicizing the legal acts; in certain circumstances, the law itself stipulates other modes of dissemination, in addition to that one, which nevertheless remains the preferred and, above all, the safest one.

Part II. The Portuguese Political System

Chapter 1. The Portuguese Democracy

§1. Portugal as a Democratic State

122. The democratic nature of the Portuguese State, despite being undisputable, is nevertheless solemnly stated in the initial precepts of the Constitutional wording.

As a matter of fact, bearing in mind that the Constitutional Revolution of 25 April 1974 was undertaken precisely in the name of democracy, we should not be surprised by the profusion of Constitutional allusions to this fact.

The democratic principle appears, consequently, in the CRP, as a general principle of Constitutional Law that pervades the entire text.

123. The Constitutional references start at once in the preamble of the CRP, which mentions explicitly the construction of a democratic State:

- 'The liberation of Portugal from dictatorship, oppression and colonialism signified a revolutionary change and the beginning of an historic turning point in Portuguese society'; and
- 'The Constituent Assembly asserts the decision of the Portuguese People to establish the basic principles of democracy'.

124. The initial precepts of the CRP, for their part, are also extremely relevant due to the various references they contain:

- 'Portugal is a sovereign republic, that is based on the will of the people' (Article 1 of the CRP);
- 'The Portuguese Republic respects the rule of law, based upon the sovereignty of the people, the pluralism of democratic expression and democratic political organization and has as its aims the deepening of participative democracy' (Article 2 of the CRP); and
- 'Sovereignty, single and indivisible, rests with the people, who shall exercise it in the manner and form laid down in this Constitution' (Article 3(1) of the CRP).

125. The political system is furthermore very intent on the preservation of democracy, which is to be upheld in the operation of the Constitutional institutions, at the State and sub-State level:

- in general terms, 'The right of democratic opposition of minorities shall be recognized on the conditions set out in this Constitution and under the Law' (Article 114(2) of the CRP);
- with regard to functional situations, the right to political argument should be underlined, for 'Political parties represented in the Assembly of the Republic, but not in the Government, have the right to broadcasting time on publicly owned radio and television, in proportion to their representation, and have the right to reply and to political argument with respect to the political statements of the government, as provided by law. The granting of the exercise of those rights shall be equivalent, in length and relevance, to that granted to the Government. Parties represented in the regional legislative assemblies shall enjoy the same rights at the level of their region' (Article 40(2) of the CRP).

Not to mention various parliamentary devices, which reflect, on the basis of each party's proportional representation in Parliament, the participation of political minorities, such as the committees of inquiry, authoritative allocation of speaking time or the allocation of the parliamentary sub-organs – the chair or the presidency of general parliamentary committees.

126. Finally, when it comes to the safeguarding of the fundamental core of the CRP, it is very clear how concerned the Constitution is about the basic features of the democratic regime, as demonstrated by some of the material limits set to its reform, for 'the laws revising the Constitution shall respect' (Article 288(d)(h) and (i) of the CRP):

- 'The rights, freedoms and guarantees of the citizens';
- 'Universal, direct, secret and regular suffrage for the selection of the elected members of the organs of government, the autonomous regions and local government and a system of proportional representation'; and
- 'Pluralism in expression and political organization, which shall include political parties and the right of democratic opposition'.

127. Throughout the text, we find abundant allusions to the democratic form of government thanks to the emphasis put on the principle of the sovereignty of the people. It is present, albeit in different degrees, in the three forms of intervention of the people in the political system that we have mentioned above:

(1) *the representative dimension*;
(2) *the dimension of the referendum (semi-direct democracy)*; and
(3) *the participative dimension.*

We shall now observe separately and in detail the relevance of each of these forms of democracy claimed by Portuguese Constitutional Law.

§2. Representative Democracy and Elections

128. The representative dimension of democracy is connected with the selection by the ruled of the rulers who discharge their mandate on behalf of the political community.

The interests they pursue are general interests, not private interests. This is why the rulers must be politically trusted by the citizens.

The bridge connecting the rulers and the ruled, at the moment of selection, is built by political representation.

129. The source of the political mandate lies here. On the basis of opposed democratic postulates, it evolved into two different models:

(1) *the imperative mandate*, claimed by Jean-Jacques Rousseau, dependent on direct democracy, where the elected should submit to the general will and could be dismissed if they violated it; and
(2) *the representative mandate*, advocated by Emmanuel Sieyès, where the elected, albeit generically submitted to the public interest, should be able to act – through their parliamentary vote, if necessary – in a manner diverging from the particular interests of their constituency or of the group of electors who had elected them, retaining their mandate even in the case of loss of political trust.

Among all the mentioned forms of democracy, representative democracy continues to be the most fundamental, notwithstanding ever-increasing arguments in favour of direct democracy in the current context of the information society: it is only through representative democracy that the capacity to act, to rationalize and to scrutinize, enabled by representation, can be achieved.

130. It is political confidence that transforms the mandate of the members of public bodies into a *representative mandate*, grounded on a particular mode of selection – elections.

Hence the fact that *popular suffrage*, operating in the selection of the persons who shall hold the offices of the State – whereby freedom to nominate candidates and the right to free electoral campaigns must be respected – consolidates the above-mentioned link of trust.

The primacy of this representative dimension is patent in Portuguese Constitutional Law where various elected bodies are to be found, not only at the State level, but also at the level of the sub-State public bodies.

And one of the initial precepts of the CRP testifies to this fact: 'The people shall exercise political power through universal, equal, direct, secret and periodic suffrage' (Article 10(1) first part of the CRP).

131. In democratic regimes election has crystallized as the central mode of selection of the holders of public office, in which the active citizens of a given State community participate through their vote.

The selection of said holders occurs by election either by way of a direct selection, or of a selection mediated by the political parties.

The relevance attributed to elections – as well as to the electorate, which subjectively carries them out – is such that it has given rise to complex questions, such as, for instance, the hypothesis of placing the electoral act on the same plane as other public law acts, in this case of the State as community. This line of thought, well represented among others by Silvestre Pinheiro Ferreira, in the nineteenth century, goes as far as connecting the electoral act to another public power – electoral power.

132. Elections as a manifestation of the electoral power held by the people do not give rise to many conceptual doubts. Consequently, they may be divided into types in accordance with the various classification criteria that are applied to them:

- *political, legislative, administrative or international elections*, depending on the nature of the organ to be elected and on its respective functions;
- *external or internal elections*, depending on whether the electoral choice is made by the people or by previously elected political bodies; and
- *general elections or by-elections* depending on whether the choice is made with regard to all the organs comprised in an institution or with regard to only one of them because the particular need to fill a vacancy has arisen.

133. The significance of the electoral act is to be found in the final act, the outcome of which is an election (the electoral result). However, it does not translate into the production of an instantaneous act, but consists of a process, in which several partial acts aimed at the production of the final act succeed one another: the election itself *stricto sensu.*

It is thus possible to distinguish between the various stages of progression of the electoral procedure, which culminate in the election itself:

- registration of the electorate on an electoral roll;
- calling of an election either as a result of the expiration of a mandate or of dissolution followed by early elections;
- nomination of candidates for election;
- the conduction of an electoral campaign aimed at providing information to the electors;
- the electoral vote;
- the counting of results;
- the settlement of electoral disputes; and
- the broadcasting of electoral results.

134. Electoral arrangements, both in purely theoretical terms, and in terms of the various choices the positive legislator can make, comprise the whole range of issues that usually arise when the time has come to regulate a given electoral process.

They are, obviously, not only concerned with the electoral system. Other matters – such as the characteristics of the suffrage, the composition of the electorate or the nomination of candidates – similarly require difficult choices between several possible alternatives.

A few other less relevant topics could be added, which in a certain fashion nevertheless influence the course of an electoral process: the conditions of registry, the rules under which political freedom by way of liberty of expression, freedom of the press and freedom of demonstration and of meeting, are exercised, the creation of parties during the election or pre-election periods and the nature of the organs entrusted with the organization and monitoring of the electoral process.

135. The electoral system – described as the method that permits the conversion into mandates of the votes cast by the citizens/electors – is, nevertheless, the most prominent of all the issues arising from the electoral arrangements.

From the technical viewpoint, the choice of an electoral system is not – and can never be – a neutral choice, since it is within that system that the structuring lines of the different instruments of political action are drawn.

Whereas with regard to the various stages of the electoral act we are usually faced merely with a legal regulation, in what concern the electoral system, the growing trend is for the Constitution to claim for itself the task of establishing its mainstays.

136. This is the reason why, among the various 'electoral topics', we have found it pertinent to expound a number of considerations about this *vexata quaestio* of all electoral arrangements.

In spite of being rooted in the unequivocal concept of the conversion of votes into mandates, this fact does not seem to prevent the electoral system from dividing itself into multiple combinations, which may fall into one of the following three categories of representation:

(1) proportional representation;
(2) majority representation; and
(3) minority representation.

§3. The Fundamental Features Of Portuguese Electoral Law

137. The relevance of elections in any democracy can also be measured against the set of normative sources of Electoral Law, a branch of Constitutional Law, the scope of which is to lay down the rules of procedure that govern it.

The task of fixing those essential principles is entrusted to the CRP that contains a specific provision in that respect, dealing with the following issues:

- registration or census of electors;
- political campaign;
- vote by suffrage;
- monitoring of electoral acts; and
- conversion of votes into mandates.

138. Among all the above topics – the complete study of which could never be really attempted in this context – we would like to focus on the choices made by Portuguese Electoral Law in respect of the three chief issues that represent the essence of an election:

(1) *electoral registration or census*;
(2) *type of suffrage*; and
(3) *electoral procedure.*

139. The electoral registration reflects an existential need to regulate the voting procedure insofar as it embodies an advanced and permanent formal attestation of each citizen's quality as elector.

In order for the citizen to be entitled to vote, he/she must obligatorily be on the electoral roll, the reason therefore being the need to avoid fraud, which is achieved through the advanced knowledge of who has a duly acknowledged active electoral ability.

The fundamental principles of electoral registration, which also apply to the holding of referendums, under Act No. 13/99, of 22 March, are the following:

- *universality*: electoral registration, on account of the universality of the suffrage, comprises all those who have an active electoral ability;
- *permanence*: whereas elections, as well as the suffrage that underpins them, possess a transient character, electoral registration is permanent and requires an organizing structure to keep it in force and ready to be updated at any time;
- *actuality*: its function being that of reflecting at each and every moment the electoral body, the registration roll must be kept up to date, the necessary changes with regard to the active voting qualification, as well as to other relevant elements, such as the electoral address, being undertaken whenever necessary;
- *the compulsory and voluntary characters*: electoral registration is compulsory for all citizens with an active voting qualification who reside on Portuguese territory, and the electoral authorities must promote said registration whenever a citizen does not take the initiative; the registration, however, is voluntary for Portuguese electors residing abroad, as well as for foreign electors who reside in Portugal; and
- *unity*: in conjunction with equality in the right to vote, there is only one registration valid for all electoral acts and referendums, every citizen being entitled to one single vote.

The duty to register the pertinent elements lies with STAPE –*Secretariado Técnico dos Assuntos para o Processo Eleitoral*, an office of the Ministry of Internal Administration, empowered to 'organize, maintain and manage the BDRE (the data bank containing the registration roll)' (Article 11(1) of Act No. 13/99).

Permanent census committees organized at the level of the parishes carry out the registration. The data collected is later used to compile the electoral rolls, which list the electors in each electoral college.

The importance of the electoral registration or census, from the viewpoint of its role towards guaranteeing the truth of any electoral act or referendum, is furthermore duly acknowledged in the type of sanctions – criminal sanctions and fines – applicable to the violation of the pertinent rules of procedure.

140. Suffrage, a term inherited from the Roman *jus sufragii*, is another critical vector of Portuguese Electoral Law as it expresses the conditions under which the individual will of the electors may be converted in a collective will asserted on election day.

According to the CRP, in a famous and often repeated sentence, suffrage is 'universal, equal, direct, secret and periodic' (Article 10(1) first part of the CRP), those qualities being, other than empty words, full of meaning from the perspective of Constitutional Law:

- *Universal suffrage*: the vote is not restricted; it extends to all those above the age of 18, who are qualified to vote. Restrictions on the ground of education, income, race, gender, belief or social status are banned.
- *Equal suffrage*: the vote being universal, all votes shall be equal, that is they shall weigh the same, the grading of their weight being prohibited. Thereby another guarantee of the plenitude of suffrage is asserted (the practice of grading the weight of votes, however, is admissible in private law institutions).
- *Direct suffrage*: the vote is projected in the choice of the candidates and no mediation scheme affects the significance of its effects, thereby ensuring that a truer expression of the will of the people is achieved.
- *Secret suffrage*: the vote is cast in privacy, the elector is never, at any moment, compelled to reveal to whom he/she has given his/her vote and is prevented from doing so within the immediate surroundings of the polling station. Greater liberty of expression is thereby achieved and pressure on certain electors on the part of the candidates is avoided.
- *Periodic suffrage*: the vote is repeated in the periods previously fixed under the electoral law insofar as political office is temporary and the holders of elective office shall be selected by a new election. This flows directly from a requirement of the republican principle.
- *Personal suffrage*: the vote is decided solely by the elector. Voting by proxy, either by choice or compulsorily is not allowed, even when the elector is prevented from voting in person owing to special circumstances. In this manner, the law ensures that the will of the elector shall never be adulterated. However, under certain circumstances, electors are entitled to vote by post, this constituting derogation from the general principle of voting in person.

Within the context of the exercise of the right to vote, the CRP makes the following further provision that seems somehow enigmatic: 'The exercise of the right to vote constitutes a civic duty' (Article 49(2) *in fine* of the CRP) and has implications in determining whether the exercise of this right can be compulsory, similar to what happens in some countries, such as Brazil or Belgium.

We are persuaded that when the Constitutional text speaks of the right to vote as a 'civic duty' it intends merely to place it on the plane of the political morality of the citizens, not to link it to a legal duty. It follows that such a duty cannot be imposed and, even less, can sanctions be brought for breach of it.

141. The electoral process exists because it assumes that an election, being a political and final public law act, is merely the outcome of a journey, which goes through several stages. In democratic political systems it has become increasingly complex. The following stages should be noted:

- *setting the date of elections*: the process starts with fixing the date when the election is to be held. This date is more or less predictable, within the calendar set in abstract by the electoral law; it is more predictable when the end of the mandate approaches and less so when the mandate ceases abruptly as a result of dissolution when the latter is legally admissible;

- *the nomination of candidates*: once the date of the election has been set, the persons and entities who wish to stand as candidates are required to present themselves before the electors, revealing their programmes;
- *electoral campaign*: once the candidates are known, a period is reserved for the electoral campaign, during which the citizens are given the opportunity to get better acquainted with the electoral programmes, habitually using extraordinary means, normally not employed outside that period;
- *organizing the polling stations*: voting is only viable if electoral officers and polling stations are arranged, this meaning the selection of persons and of the locations where the vote shall be cast, the number of citizens being distributed among the various locations according to their electoral residence;
- *vote*: this is the moment when each elector exercises his/her right to vote choosing from among the various alternatives personified by the different candidates;
- *counting the results*: in the first stage, this is carried out at the polling station and later carried out in wider terms, in order to convert the votes into mandates under rules of its own that are inherent to the nature of each body to be elected; and
- *settlement of electoral disputes*: once the votes have been cast and counted, any irregularity may be brought before the courts since it is legitimate to bring before the judiciary acts that are considered illegal or violate the Constitution.

§4. Semi-direct Democracy and the Referendum

142. Referendum in a democracy is the possibility for the citizens to express their opinion on government matters.

The issue is no longer the selection of political rulers, on the basis of their personal capabilities or of their political ideas, rulers who, once elected, shall hold the responsibility of deciding for the people.

With a referendum it is the people who decide, for themselves, certain matters by intervening on given occasions in the resolution of public affairs. Momentarily the people, that is, the entire body of ruled citizens, transform themselves into ruling people and settle the questions that have been put to them.

143. The political device provided by the Constitution to implement semi-direct democracy is the referendum, the act by which the people answer a question put to them concerning a matter requiring a decision on the part of the rulers.

The will expressed in a referendum –'yes', 'no' or 'abstention'– gives voice to the people's opinion, which is collectively valid.

Holding a referendum implies that the people shall decide on a matter, which is normally entrusted to the representative bodies.

The word 'referendum' (*ad referendum*) has been borrowed from international public law, within which framework treaties are negotiated *ad referendum* if they must be subsequently submitted for approval/ratification to the competent national authorities. In this case, a parallel is drawn with regard to the question that is put to the people, which requires subsequent acceptance or rejection.

The CRP acknowledges exactly the foregoing description when it enshrines the referendum and emphasizes the relevance of this device for the enrichment of Portuguese democracy: 'The people shall exercise political power by suffrage by way of referendum and of the other forms laid down in this Constitution' (Article 10(1) of the CRP).

144. An examination of how the Constitution deals with the referendum offers a variety of approaches that are relevant in order to apply to this device the existing classifications:

- *the matters on which a referendum may be held*: Constitutional, international, political, legislative and administrative referendum;
- *the moment when it is held*: in advance, final or supervening;
- *the mandatory or non-mandatory character of the call*: mandatory or non-mandatory referendum; and
- *the legal force of the answer*: binding referendum and consultative referendum.

145. The referendum has probably been one of the topics in Constitutional Law that has given rise, over the last decades, to the liveliest debates in this field, following increasingly sharper analyses, which have also provided political science with meaningful insights into the topic.

It is a fact that contemporary democracy was born to a large extent as an alternative to the referendum democracy that carries, furthermore, the heavy historical burden of rather undemocratic experiences.

But it is equally true that the information society in which we live requires a larger participation of the citizens and that the difficulties and risks associated with the referendum have been gradually overcome.

The problem of technical ignorance of the respective subject matter on the part of the people who are going to decide is no longer a relevant concern because the decisions are piecemeal decisions and it has become mandatory to conduct a large information campaign before the referendum.

The question of the distortion of the outcome of the referendum to give it the character of a plebiscite is purely theoretical since the referendum is not an island; on the contrary, it exists in a globally democratic context, where it cohabits with other instruments of political participation and lives side by side with electoral democracy.

And we would like to advance a step further: at a time when many believe that democracy is going through a profound crisis as a result of either a general distrust of politicians, or of the inability of the representative and partisan instruments to give adequate answers to people's concerns, the referendum could be an important security valve and provide a minimum of democratic oxygen to the political system.

§5. Fundamental Elements of the Portuguese Law on Referendums

146. The referendum has not always existed in Portuguese Constitutional Law; it was only adopted in the wake of Constitutional reform. Three different types of referendums were adopted at three different times:

(1) *Local referendum in 1982*, enshrined in Constitutional Amendment Act No. 1/1982, which asserts that 'Local authorities may subject to referendum by their electors matters falling within the powers of their respective bodies' (Article 240(1) of the CRP).
- *National referendum in 1989*, enshrined in Constitutional Amendment Act No. 1/1989, which establishes that 'Electors registered in the national census may be called upon to give their opinion directly in a referendum called by decision of the President of the Republic, following a proposal by Parliament or the government, on matters within the respective powers of these organs' (Article 115(1) of the CRP); one of these matters is the establishment of the administrative regions (Article 256 of the CRP).
- *Regional referendum in 1997*, enshrined in Constitutional Amendment Act No. 1/1997, to be held in the autonomous regions. It stipulates, 'the referendums may have a regional scope' (Article 115(13) of the CRP) and 'it rests with the legislative assembly of the pertinent autonomous region to propose questions to be put in a regional referendum, whereby electors residing in the respective territory may, by decision of the President of the Republic, be called upon to give their opinion directly and with binding force on issues of a relevant specific regional interest' (Article 232(2) of the CRP).

147. Two ordinary laws, one concerning the national referendum, passed in 1998 (LORR), and the other concerning local referendum, passed in 2000 Local Referendum Organic Law (LORL), have amply developed the rules and regulations under which the referendums operate. The first of these laws comprises 255 articles, organized as follows:

- Chapter I – *General Principles.*
- Chapter II – *Calling a Referendum.*
- Chapter III – *Holding a Referendum.*
- Chapter IV – *Effects of the Referendum.*
- Chapter V – *Special Rules Concerning the Referendum on the Establishment of Concrete Administrative Regions.*
- Chapter VI – *Miscellaneous and Transitory Provisions.*

It is regrettable that, up to the present time, no law has been passed for the purpose of regulating by ordinary law the regional referendum and it is doubtful whether it will suffice to refer to the provisions concerning national referendum.

On the contrary, in light of some of those issues, the general character of the Electoral Law with regard to the law on referendums has been asserted (Article 115(9) of the CRP).

By virtue of its compulsory intervention under the system of preventive judiciary review of constitutionality and legality, Constitutional jurisprudence has repeatedly had the opportunity to intervene and adjudicate on the referendum system, both at the national and the local level.

148. The *national referendum* is the instrument that has the highest number of provisions, as required by the prominent place it occupies within the scope of strengthening Portuguese political democracy.

Until now, three national referenda have been held, two in the same year of 1998 and the third quite recently, in 2007:

(1) the first on 28 June 1998, on the question of abortion on request, when the 'no' vote won;
(2) the second on 8 November 1998, on administrative regionalization of the continental territory, the outcome of which was also the victory of the 'no' vote; and
(3) the third on 11 February 2007, again on the issue of decriminalization of abortion, with victory this time for the 'yes' vote.

Currently another referendum has been put on hold: the referendum on the ratification of the Reforming Treaty of Lisboa by Portugal. To this effect, and in order to avoid disputes, the Constitution was submitted to a seventh reform procedure in 2005. Under a new amendment, it is now possible to hold a direct referendum on the text of the Treaty on European Union by way of a question regarding its ratification or non-ratification.

149. According to the text of the CRP, the national referendum 'can only be held on issues of relevant national interest, that fall within the powers of decision of either Parliament or the government by way of their consent to an international convention or the enactment of legislation' (Article 115(3) of the CRP).

With regard to the subject matters, the general notion that they must be 'issues of relevant national interest' ensures a positive delimitation; this is an indeterminate concept, to be construed by the bodies intervening in the procedure, yet it allows issues not worthy of a national referendum to be banned.

The CRP and the LORR go a bit further when it comes to the densification of that general concept and, at the formal level, they frame the scope of the referendum, limiting it to those matters 'that fall within the powers of decision of either Parliament or the Government by virtue of the approval of an international convention or the enactment of legislation' (Article 2 of the LORR).

It should be noted that this clarification regarding the definition of the matters that can be subject to referendum leads to the exclusion of issues that can only be decided by acts of another nature – such as Constitutional, political, administrative or judicial acts, as well as legislation that does not fall within the powers of those two organs of government, such as the acts of the legislative assemblies of the autonomous regions, or in other words, the regional legislative decrees.

On the contrary, many matters appear, in light of the CRP's concern with setting a negative delimitation regarding issues that may be subject to a national referendum, to have been expressly banned as already hinted at, in some cases, in the course of the positive delimitation:

- amendments to the Constitution;
- budgetary, fiscal and financial matters and actions;
- matters within the exclusive powers reserved to Parliament; and

- matters within the powers reserved absolutely to Parliament, with a few specific exceptions.

150. The universe of citizens who have the right to vote in a national referendum corresponds in a large measure to the citizens who are entitled to vote at elections.

The general rule is that in a national referendum the right to vote is confined to those 'electors registered on national territory', this registration being compulsory.

Notwithstanding the above general rule, the law allows citizens with an active qualification to vote, who are registered abroad, to vote as long as the referendums are held 'on issues that also concern them specifically' (Article 115(12) of the CRP).

151. The calling of a national referendum is not an instantaneous act; it follows a procedure consisting of the three following stages:

(1) *the proposal*: by Parliament or the Government depending on whether the act at issue falls within the powers of one or the other of these organs of government; in the first case, the initiative rests with the deputies or the parliamentary political groups, in the second case with the government and groups of electors, the minimum number of which must be 75,000 Portuguese electors;
(2) *the preventive judiciary review of constitutionality and legality*: after the question has been formulated, it is submitted to a compulsory judicial review for the purpose of scrutinizing its compliance with the Constitution and the law, as well as with the requirements in respect of the eligible electorate. It falls to the President of the Republic to forward the proposal to the Constitutional Court for the purpose of preventive judiciary review. The Court must take a decision within a normal period of twenty-five days, that can, however, be shortened on grounds of urgency. The decision of the Court may be positive or negative with regard to the proposal at issue; and
(3) *the decision*: if the Constitutional Court declares that the proposed question complies with the Constitution and the law, the President of the Republic has discretionary powers to take a decision with respect to the holding of the referendum (there is no decision if the proposed question is ruled to be unconstitutional or unlawful; in that case the question shall be reformulated); if the president's decision is affirmative, he/she has twenty days to call the referendum by decree, an act that also fixes the date when it shall be held.

152. Once a referendum has been called the conduction and implementation stages begin. This is the stage where people express their will and it consists of several steps:

- *The campaign*: it corresponds to the period prior to the date of the vote, during which time public information events are organized aimed at convincing the voters about the alternative answers. The political parties are entitled to take part in these events.
- *The organization of the polling places (assembleias de voto)*: it is related to the administrative organization of the exercise of the right to vote and the setting up of polling places to which all voters within a circumscribed geographic territory

are assigned, in order to ensure the efficiency and veracity of their political expression, as well as to guarantee freedom and impartiality.
- *The casting of the vote*: the instant when each voting citizen expresses his/her will to answer, in one of the possible senses, the question put in the referendum.
- *The determination of the results*: this means counting the votes and includes the procedures for challenging the results.

The holding of a national referendum is usually optional as there is no requirement to call one in order to decide on any political or legislative issue.

The only exception to this is the matter of administrative regionalization, any decision on which is subject to the calling and passage of a referendum: 'The establishment of each administrative region, which shall be provided for by the respective law of establishment, shall depend on the law referred to in Article 255 and on a favourable vote by a majority of the electorate that has given its opinion in direct consultations, of national scope and relating to each regional area' (Article 256(1) of the CRP).

153. The *effects* of a national referendum are binding since it would not be reasonable to hold such a major consultation for purely consultative purposes.

However, for the referendum to be legally binding, a minimum turnout is further required: 'The referendum shall be binding only if the number of voters turning out to vote is higher than 50% of the voters registered on the electoral registers' (Article 115(11) of the CRP).

The binding force of the referendum is assessed against two types of duties that emerge from its outcome and which are projected onto the actions of the bodies legally and politically empowered to take action in this respect:

(1) *A positive duty* to *facere*, to act: the duty to enact the appropriate law providing for the implementation of the decision voted by referendum – or, as the law puts it, to enact a law with 'a corresponding sense' – within ninety or sixty days, depending on whether the duty lies with Parliament or with the government. At the same time, restrictions are laid down relating to the presidential powers following a rationale of *faculté d'empêcher*.
(2) *A negative duty* to *non facere*, not to act: the duty not to pass legislation contrary to the sense of the decision voted by referendum, a negative duty which ceases in case of 'a new election for Parliament or the holding of a new referendum with a negative outcome'.

According to the rationale of the national referendum, and in contrast to other Constitutional systems, the decision taken by a referendum vote is not a direct source of law, but rather an impulse to make law, that is to make the corresponding laws and international treaties. This is why we should dismiss the opinions that enhance excessively the outcome of a referendum.

A referendum is:

- *a political act*, performed by the people who, gathered on the day it is held, represent its formal author. It is an act of the State as a community;

- *with cogent effects*, of a normative nature, given that the result of the vote, if the voter participation is higher than half the registered voters, is binding in accordance with the CRP and the LORR; and
- *but only with internal efficacy* since it does not, of itself alone, affect the establishment, amendment or extinction of other public law acts.

154. The *local referendum* is an instrument that assumes a lesser political importance insofar as it is limited to administrative issues pertaining to the local authorities where it is held. Nevertheless it has Constitutional status, albeit minor, and a very extensive legal status under the LORL.

The local referendum has the following main features and is carried out within the scope of the parishes (*freguesias*) and districts (*municípios*), which are public bodies of an administrative nature:

- The *object* of the referendum is restricted to matters of local interest that fall within the powers and competences of the local authorities.
- The *holding* of a referendum is always optional and no decision on administrative policy depends on it to be made. The decision does not depend on the calling of a referendum.
- The *initiative* to call a referendum lies with the local authorities and with the citizens entitled to vote, by way of a citizens' initiative, although the final decision is the responsibility of the deliberative organs of the local authorities, the municipal council (*assembleia municipal*) or the parish council (*assembleia de freguesia*). This is followed by the mandatory judicial review of the constitutionality and legality of the decision.
- The *effects* of the referendum are legally binding, never merely advisory, and the local authorities must respect the result, their duty being either positive or negative depending on the sense of the vote.

§6. Participative Democracy and Political Parties

155. The participative dimension of democracy, less organic and more informal, is the dimension connected with the exercise of rights of a political nature, which enable the expression of a *public opinion* exerting an indirect influence on the political decisions taken by the Government and the other ruling bodies. Public opinion is formed on the basis of individual opinions freely produced in the public arena.

We mean by this that the popular will that must be taken into consideration by any political system is not limited to whatsoever is transmitted at the moment of the election or of the referendum. The citizens' opinions that might be expressed between the said formal moments of decision are equally important for they give substance to a democratic culture and represent an active intervention of society in the issues of politics.

This other facet of democracy is not carried out against, and much less in replacement of, representative democracy; it is quite clear, however, that participative democracy complements representative democracy and denotes a healthy democratic scrutiny of the day-to-day activities of political governance.

Hence the importance of examining the two main functions performed by public opinion in a democracy:

(1) A *legitimizing function*: the function that enables the factual and ethical acceptance of the actions of the Government and the other ruling bodies considering that the latter may absorb the dominant social conceptions reflected in public opinion, thereby avoiding a divorce between the State and society.
(2) A *function of scrutiny*: the limitation of public power flows from this function insofar as, in contrast to the theory of the *arcana rei publicae* of the absolute State, it is required that the electors assess the circumstances in which political decisions are made and, as a result, are in a better position to pass judgment on the rulers at elections, while, for their part, the latter are conditioned by the scrutiny of public opinion.

156. The instruments put at the service of this participative democracy are all connected with *political rights*, which, in turn, are all part of an ideal political status of active citizenship that participate in the public arena in the construction of public opinion.

Several basic civil rights may exemplify that notion, thus conferring substance on a public opinion that, when it is strong, enhances participative democracy, forming a crucial component of an advanced and mature democratic State:

- *Freedom of expression* (expression and information): the liberty for citizens freely to express their points of view on all sorts of issues, without being coerced, censored or discriminated (Article 37 of the CRP).
- *Press freedom*: the right of citizens to express their free opinions by way of the media – the press, the traditional media, radio and television – and also the faculty, equally comprised in this fundamental right, to create these media, a right that extends to journalists in their capacity as media professionals (Articles 38 and 39 of the CRP).
- *Freedom of assembly*: the right of citizens to assemble freely for the exchange of ideas or to carry out some project (Article 45(1) of the CRP).
- *The right to demonstrate*: the right of people to gather freely in order to broadcast their viewpoints outside their own group (Article 45(2) of the CRP).
- *The right of freedom of association*: the right to freely create, in the exercise of private autonomy, bodies corporate or unincorporated associations without requiring any kind of authorization (Article 46 of the CRP).
- *The right to establish or join political parties*: the right of people to establish and join political parties, and to work jointly towards their ends, taking part in their activities; the same right extends to the parties in their capacity as special associations (Article 51 of the CRP).
- *The right of petition before public bodies*: the right of people to present to public authorities requests, representations, claims or complaints regarding their rights,

the law in general or for the purpose of furthering public interest (Article 52 of the CRP).

157. The status of the *democratic opposition* constitutes a further link between representative democracy and participative democracy, considering that in a democratic State if the duty of the majority is to govern, it is the duty of the minorities to conduct scrutiny of government policies.

This is why we approve of the CRP's provision for a formal status of democratic opposition that comprises a range of procedural rights granted to the minorities in public bodies of a representative nature, at the national, regional and local level, among which we would like to point out the following:

- *The right to be informed*: this right is at the core of the right of opposition and it includes the 'right to be regularly and directly informed by the pertinent executive bodies about the progress of the chief matters of public interest relating to their activities'.
- *The right to prior consultation*: this is a stronger right and grants to its holders the possibility of giving their opinion before certain major decisions are made.
- *The right of participation*: 'the right to speak their opinion on and intervene in any matter of major public interest making use of the available Constitutional and legal means, as well as the right to attend and participate in all the official acts and ceremonies, the nature of which so justifies it'.
- *The right to participate in lawmaking*: the 'right to give their opinion while the government is drafting legislative proposals' on matters relating to 'elections and political associations and parties'.
- *The right to appear and be heard*: the right to 'appear before and be heard by any committee set up for the purpose of producing white papers and reports, conducting inquiries, inspections, investigations and other forms of inquiry on matters of major national, regional or local interest'.

158. Of all the fundamental rights of political intervention, as Georg Jellinek would put it, the right to partisan association, or in other words, the phenomenon of *political parties* and all that is implied by it, deserves a special mention even though the freedom of the media, in our current information society, cannot be ignored either.

All sorts of authors have attempted to define political parties on the basis of diverging criteria. In Portugal, the notion of political party was one of the main concerns of the first LPP – enacted by Decree-Law No. 595/74, of 7 November, which stated that 'By political parties are meant the organizations of citizens, with a permanent character, formed with the fundamental objective of democratic participation in the political life of the country and of contributing, in accordance with the Constitutional laws and their published statutes and programmes, to the formation and expression of the political will of the people, namely by their intervention in the electoral process by way of the nomination or support of candidates.'

This old legal definition can be useful because, taking it as the point of departure, it is possible to isolate the elements which are generally considered by doctrine to form the concept of political party either under Constitutional Law or in keeping with a political science approach:

- a *subjective element*;
- a *temporal element*; and
- a *teleological element*.

The *subjective element*, as suggested by the aforementioned Portuguese law, when it refers to political parties as 'organizations of citizens', implies that a personal dimension underpins the entity to be created. In contrast to the case of foundations or societies, this personal element – which is then present, in different gradations, in the party members and party supporters – confers to parties the qualification of associations.

The *temporal element* presupposes that political parties shall have an enduring character. This means that parties, in light of their objectives, as well as of the social and political function they perform, cannot be created for a fixed term or under some condition. The existence of a stable organization is one feature of parties that distinguishes them from other groups that have purely electoral purposes.

The *teleological element* emphasizes the purposes of the political parties. It relates to the acknowledgement by the law of the important part played by political parties in the operation of the representative system enshrined in the Constitution.

In brief, we may define political parties as *bodies corporate of the associative type, having a permanent character, the purpose of which is to represent the State/ Society at the level of the public power organs, thus contributing, as fundamental pieces, towards the operation of the current system of political power.*

§7. The New Political Parties Law in Portugal

159. We have just observed how, since the nineteenth century and up to the present day, a path has been gradually trodden which has lead towards the acknowledgement by the law of the political parties. Nowadays, in the legal orders of the various states, this is a clear and an unequivocal fact, both with regard to ordinary law and the Constitution.

Peculiarly, in Portuguese law, the incorporation of political parties within the Constitution was preceded by the enactment, in the revolutionary period, of Decree-Law No. 595/74, of 7 November, the former LPP, which stayed in force until quite recently albeit with a few amendments. The above-mentioned law established the global legal regime of political parties, at a time when, following the Constitutional Revolution of 25 April 1974, they were rapidly proliferating.

However, in 2003, this legislation was replaced by a new law – the new LPP – which remodelled many of its features: in addition to the notion of political parties and to their differentiation from political associations, other critical aspects were regulated, among which were the formation and the extinction of political parties.

We are now faced with a more comprehensive and up-to-date legal conception, clearly visible in its forty-one articles distributed across six chapters:

(1) Chapter I – *Basic principles.*
(2) Chapter II – *Formation and Extinction.*
(3) Chapter III – *Members.*
(4) Chapter IV – *Internal Organization.*
(5) Chapter V – *Activities and Means of Organization.*
(6) Chapter VI – *Final Provisions.*

160. The CRP also took care to assert the status of the parties, accepting their role within the political system. This matter appears in various Constitutional precepts, in the key regulatory parts of the CRP:

- *in the introductory principles*;
- *in the fundamental rights*; and
- *in the organization of political power.*

Examples of this are two Constitutional provisions that encapsulate in general, within the current Portuguese Constitutional system, the function of the political parties:

(1) One provision contained in the fundamental principles proclaims, 'The political parties shall assist in bringing about the organization and expression of the will of the people and shall respect the principles of national independence, the unity of the State and political democracy' (Article 10(2) of the CRP).
(2) Another provision in the part relating to the fundamental rights states that: 1. Freedom of association includes the right to establish or join political parties, and, through them, to work jointly and democratically to give expression to the will of the people and to organize political power; (Article 51(1) of the CRP).

The above-mentioned provisions make clear the movement operated by the CRP resulting in a *formal incorporation* of the political parties. There was the intention of taking a stand against the regime ousted in 1974, that had fascist leanings and rejected political pluralism, by expressly incorporating that institution, and, above all, by trying to enshrine its status in a comprehensive manner.

161. The key features of that Constitutional regime are, in brief, the following:

- Only an external scrutiny of the activity of the parties is stipulated and not a scrutiny of their programme or statutes, such scrutiny being entrusted to the courts, specifically to the Constitutional Court.
- As results from an analysis of the above-mentioned provisions, the CRP, as had the LPP of 1974, recognizes the aims and purposes of the political parties within the framework of the current political system, namely their representative function and the fact that they hold political power, as well as their relevant function in contributing to the formation of the 'popular will'.
- With regard to the representative function, the political parties are given a monopoly in the nomination of candidates to the organs of political power at the national level – Parliament and European Parliament – and at the regional level – legislative assemblies of the autonomous regions.

- The CRP also contains provisions concerning parliamentary political groups and acknowledges the right of opposition to the parties represented in Parliament, but not in the government, as well as the right to broadcasting time, right of reply and right to political debate.

162. We would also like to point out an important limit imposed by the CRP on the aims of the parties, prohibiting them from embracing a 'fascist or racist ideology' (Article 46(4) of the CRP), and admitting the possibility of extinction of the party should that reality occur.

Indeed, and so that the importance of this topic may become evident, a law prohibiting fascist organizations is still in force. Act No. 64/78, of 6 October, lays down a very comprehensive prohibition. Bent on overcoming merely formal obstacles, it extends considerably the prohibition along the lines of the three central points below:

(1) *the professed fascist ideology*:
[A]ny organization which, by its statutes, manifestos and communiqués, by the statements of its leaders or officials or by its actions, show that it has adopted, advocates, intends to disseminate or actually disseminates the values, principles, exponents, institutions and methods, which distinguish the fascist regimes recorded in history, namely bellicose rhetoric, violence as a form of political combat, colonialism, racism, corporativism, or the exaltation of the most representative personalities of those regimes, shall be considered to profess fascism;
(2) *the activities addressed*:
[A]ny observable conjunction or convergence of efforts and wills, with or without the help of material means, having a legal existence, regardless of its form, or merely a de facto existence, with a permanent or a merely temporary character, shall be considered an organization;
(3) *the people within its reach*:
[A]ny person who has organized or held relevant office in an organization that has been declared extinct on the ground that it professes the fascist ideology shall be punished with imprisonment of two to eight years.

163. Many of the provisions of the LPP attest to the importance of the Constitutional status of the political parties, namely the initial one that, in a large measure, takes up and reproduces their Constitutional function, conferring on them the task of contributing to bringing about 'the free formation and pluralism of expression of the people's will and the organization of political power, with respect for the principles of national independence, the unity of the State and political democracy'.

A large number of the other basic principles included in the LPP serve the same purpose:

- the principle of indeterminate duration;
- the principle of freedom, both with regard to their formation and to the development of their activities;
- the principle of democracy in their internal organization;
- the principle of transparency with respect to their activities; and

– the principle of their national character.

164. With regard to their formation, it follows from the principle of freedom that the birth of a political party does not require any kind of official authorization: 'The formation of a political party is free and not subject to authorization.'

Notwithstanding, the law stipulates some formal conditions that are to be met if the political party is to exist and in the absence of which it cannot operate: the submission of a request signed by a minimum of 7,500 voters with the draft statutes attached, the statement of principles or the political programme, as well as the denomination, acronym and symbol of the party.

The legal identity of the political parties and the commencement of their activity result from their registration with the Constitutional Court, under a system of prior declaration by simple registration, the latter not being accepted should any of the above-mentioned formal requisites be missing.

Regarding the extinction of political parties, it is duly regulated under two different perspectives: voluntary extinction, referred to as dissolution, and forced extinction, which is equivalent to judicial extinction:

(1) *Voluntary extinction* is the extinction of the political party by decision of its organs, with the Constitutional Court having to be informed of the decision for the purpose of cancelling the registration.
(2) *Judicial extinction* is the extinction of the political party, ordained by the Constitutional Court following ascertainment of the factors that determine the extinction, all of the latter being formal. In no circumstances shall the material activity carried out by the political party be interfered with.

165. The new LPP, for its part, also deals with the status of members of political parties, laying down a significant set of rules regarding their relations with the partisan structures.

The importance of party members is enormous because they are the ones who form the infrastructure underpinning the party, both at the outset, when they join together and organize themselves in order to launch a new party, and, after its formation, when they instil life into the party thanks to their political activities and the conviction they project in the professed doctrine and programme.

The freedom of party association is usually viewed from the institutional standpoint of the political parties. However the LPP also focuses on the individual dimension, that is to say on the relation between each citizen and each political party: 'No one shall be compelled to join or not to join any political party, or compelled, by any means, to remain affiliated.'

Party affiliation, even if conceived with the greatest liberty, implies limitations, some of them natural and some derived from the status of the citizens with regard to other public bodies:

– *Impossibility of being affiliated with two parties*: members of one party cannot, simultaneously, be affiliated with another party.

– *Restrictions on party membership*: citizens with certain given status are subject to limitations on their partisan activity, being prevented from holding certain party offices, or, in some circumstances, establishing a party affiliation.

166. With regard to their inner structure, general freedom of organization is the rule. This reflects on the institutional plane the principle of freedom of party association.

Nevertheless, the LPP lays down some important rules, to which it applies, in some cases, the general rules that govern public bodies.

A distinction may be drawn between national organs and other organs. Among the former, meanwhile, one should distinguish between the representative organ, the party direction and the dispute-settling organ, not to mention the hypothesis, left open, of holding internal referendums.

Within the internal organization the most important role is played by the organs of political direction and the executive organs, which direct the party, implementing the decisions made by the representative organs, answering any complaints forwarded by the rank and file and developing the party's political strategy in light of the issues that arise at all times in national political life.

The executive organs may be collegiate, as is the case with committees and councils, or single, namely the presidency of the party entrusted to a single person on the ground that history has proved the need for strong and appealing, even charismatic, leadership that will become the party's image.

Internal elections are held by personal and secret vote and the results are always open to appeal before the Constitutional Court; this must be preceded by the lodging of a claim with the internal dispute-settling organ.

167. Every party may adopt the internal organization of their choice and citizens are at full liberty to join or not join the existing political parties.

On the part of the State there is no scrutiny of the internal workings of parties, as the CRP and the LPP limit themselves to setting external and formal mechanisms for the scrutiny of the parties' activity and organization.

Notwithstanding, it has been debated whether parties should not, in their internal organization, be compelled to abide by certain more demanding requirements of the democratic principle or, on the contrary, whether the State should keep a neutral stance in this matter. This is a crucial issue, which the Constitutional Court was faced with when it was called upon to review, under a procedure of preventive judicial review, the new LPP. The Court decided on the three following points:

(1) judicial extinction on the ground that the periodical nomination of candidates has not occurred;
(2) the need to adopt the principle of secret vote at internal elections and referendums; and
(3) removal from internal offices.

We have already noted that the CRP – like the LF in its Article 21 – compels parties to abide by the democratic principle in their Grundgesetz internal organization. This flows from the terms of its Article 51(5): 'Political parties shall be governed by the principles of transparency, democratic organization and management and participation of all of their members.'

168. The current landscape of Portuguese political life comprises eighteen political parties. However, it should not be assumed that the Portuguese system, from the viewpoint of its representation, is a perfect multiparty system where all the parties have the same significance. Rather it should be viewed as an *imperfect and polarized multiparty system* where only seven of those parties are represented in Parliament, on the basis of the electoral results of the latest legislative elections of June 2011.

Chapter 2. Portuguese Organs of Government

§1. The President of the Republic

169. The CRP has opted to place in the first of the sections dealing with the organs of government the provisions relating to the President of the Republic, conferring five basic duties of office: 'The President of the Republic shall represent the Portuguese Republic, guarantee the independence of the nation, the unity of the State and the proper functioning of the democratic institutions and shall be, ex officio, the Commander-in-chief of the Armed Forces' (Article 120 of the CRP).

These five Constitutional tasks entrusted to the Head of State are, basically, a summary of the powers he/she holds within the context of a semi-presidential government system.

But it is also a definition of a largely declaratory nature, aimed at introducing the reader to the description of the President of the Republic in the CRP, which dedicates Section II of Part III, with three chapters, to that topic:

(1) Chapter I – *Status and Election.*
(2) Chapter II – *Powers.*
(3) Chapter III – *Council of State.*

170. The President of the Republic, an organ consisting of one single person, exercises a five-year term of office; he/she is barred from seeking re-election to a third consecutive term 'during the five years following immediately the end of a second consecutive term of office' (Article 123(1) of the CRP).

The selection of the President of the Republic is based on 'universal, direct and secret suffrage by Portuguese citizens who are registered as voters in the national territory, as well as Portuguese citizens resident abroad' (Article 121(1) of the CRP).

Passive entitlement to vote, by contrast to active entitlement, is rather limited since it only comprises:

- Portuguese citizens of both sexes, under the condition that they are;
- Portuguese citizens by descent;
- at least 35 years of age (Article 122 of the CRP), the discrimination on the ground of age being hardly understandable in light of the principle of equality and the republican principle.

The voting system is majoritarian (Article 126 of the CRP), in two rounds; in the first round the winner is the candidate who obtains more than half the votes cast, a second round being required if this does not happen; in the latter case, the winner is the candidate who receives the greater number of votes, one of the candidates obtaining an absolute majority of votes with respect to the other.

The President of the Republic, if he/she is temporarily unable or in case of vacancy of the office, shall be replaced in the discharge of his/her functions by the President of the Assembly of the Republic (Article 132 of the CRP), regardless of a few limitations to the exercise of the presidential powers notwithstanding the principle of correspondence between the powers of both organs: (i) acts he/she can only perform after prior consultative advice of the Council of State and (ii) acts he/ she is not permitted to perform (Article 139 of the CRP).

The President of the Republic is free to resign from his/her office at any time without having to seek prior material authorization, although formal notice must be given to the Assembly of the Republic. The resignation must be subsequently published in the official journal (Article 131(1) of the CRP). Should he/she resign his/ her office, however, then 'he shall not stand for office either at the immediately following election or at elections held in the five-year period after the resignation' (Article 123(2) of the CRP).

171. When it comes to the powers of the Head of State, and in contrast to the powers of the Assembly of the Republic and the Government, where the approach is based on a material division, the Constitution distinguishes between powers as follows:

- 'Powers relating to other organs';
- 'Powers to act'; and
- 'Powers in international relations'.

Unfortunately this is merely a formal distribution of powers that says little about the essence of each of them. Focusing on them as a whole we will see that the Head of State performs actions of the most diverse type:

- *Actions of an international nature*, relating to the international life of the State.
- *Actions of a government nature*, relating to the workings of the system of government and to participation in the lawmaking process.
- *Actions of an administrative nature*, relating to the military institution and to its administration.

172. The 'powers relating to other organs' may be grouped around three different poles, featuring aspects of the workings of the other organs:

(1) to preside over Constitutional organs;
(2) to intervene in the composition of organs by setting the dates for the election of their members, by appointing other office holders and by ordering the dissolution of said organs; and
(3) to take part in their activity by addressing messages to them, should circumstances arise that might so justify it.

The most relevant of these features is the second and, in that respect, we would like to point out the dissolution of the Assembly of the Republic, the dismissal of the Government and the appointment of the prime minister and of the Government.

The dissolution of the Assembly of the Republic is, according to the wording of the Constitution, a free or discretionary power, the opportunity of which can only be assessed by the President of the Republic. In practice, it is a power that, on account of its weight, is only used as a last resort, when confronted with two ultimate situations, that is, when, in the absence of a stable majority, which could be a coalition between various parties, the formation of a lasting government becomes unviable; and when, despite the existence of such a majority, the lack of political legitimacy of that same majority and of the Government it supports is demonstrable.

The Government's dismissal occurs under the following conditions: 'The President of the Republic may dismiss the government when it becomes necessary in order to guarantee the proper functioning of the democratic institutions and after prior consultation of the Council of State' (Article 195(2) of the CRP).

Despite the fact that the concept is vague, the justification behind this power to dismiss the government lies in the endangerment, as a result of the Government's activity, of the CRP, political freedom, the separation of powers or democracy itself, in a stage of transition towards a pre-dictatorial regime.

This is why it is no longer a political responsibility as it was until 1982, but an institutional responsibility deriving from the Constitutional design of the status and powers of the various organs.

The appointment of the prime minister and the dismissal of the Government are, by contrast to the dissolution of the Assembly of the Republic, relatively restricted powers, in part because the CRP limits them by stipulating that the President of the Republic shall seek the opinion of the parties represented in Parliament and consider the electoral results (Article 190(1) of the CRP), but mostly because it depends basically on the political majority in the Parliament.

The amount of manoeuvring space conceded to the President of the Republic, however, can be extended when there are no majorities of a single party or of a coalition. In that case he/she is in a position to perform a leading role in fostering the necessary coalitions, starting precisely with the choice of the proper person for prime minister.

173. The 'powers to act' comprise a vast array of powers of a political nature, among which the following should be noted:

- participation in the various lawmaking procedures, such as promulgation and political veto;
- calling of national referendums following an initiative by the Assembly of the Republic or of the Government;
- declaration of a state of exception; and
- exercise of the power of clemency, through pardon or the commutation of sentences.

The 'powers in international relations' are narrower and aimed at asserting the position of the Head of State as the representative of sovereignty. They entail three specific actions (Article 135 of the CRP):

(1) the appointment of ambassadors and extraordinary envoys, as well as the accreditation of foreign diplomatic representatives;
(2) the ratification of solemn international treaties following their approval; and

(3) the declaration of a state of war after prior authorization by the Assembly of the Republic and consultation with the Council of State.

§2. Assembly of the Republic

174. The *Assembly of the Republic*, which is systematically located in the CRP after the Head of State, is a unicameral and collective organ, with a pluralist party-political basis.

The Constitutional text regulates this organ extensively. Three chapters included in Section III of Part III of the CRP deal with it:

(1) Chapter I – Status and Election.
(2) Chapter II – Powers.
(3) Chapter III – Organization and Operation.

The nature of the Assembly of the Republic is that of a representative organ of the Portuguese people as stated in the CRP itself: 'The Assembly of the Republic is the representative assembly of all Portuguese citizens' (Article 147 of the CRP).

In light of its organizational and functional complexity, the legal status of the Assembly of the Republic is amply described, in addition to the numerous Constitutional provisions, in the Standing Orders of the Assembly of the Republic with 292 Articles carrying the following titles:

- Title I – Deputies and Parliamentary Political Groups.
- Title II – Organization of the Assembly.
- Title III – Operations.
- Title IV – Procedures.
- Title V – Other Orders.

175. As its name denotes, the Assembly of the Republic is a parliamentary-type collegial organ consisting of deputies, the number of whom is limited between a minimum and a maximum, set out under the electoral law in the following terms: 'The Assembly of the Republic shall have not less than one hundred and eighty and not more than two hundred and thirty deputies' (Article 148 of the CRP).

The current electoral law has opted for the maximum limit and, as a result, there are 230 elected deputies. The voting system is one of proportional representation, with counting by the d'Hondt method.

The distribution of the assembly's electorate across the electoral districts is partially linked to the existing twenty-two districts:

- *electoral districts* that comprise the voters registered in Continental Portugal administrative districts, one for each of the existing eighteen districts;
- *regional electoral districts*, comprising the voters registered in the archipelagos of the Azores and Madeira; and

- *emigration electoral districts* where only voters registered outside Portugal are authorized to vote; there is one district for Europe and another for outside of Europe.

The distribution of the deputies to be elected by each of these electoral districts, under the provisions of the electoral law, varies depending on the density of registered voters, except in the emigration electoral districts, which only elect four deputies. There is a further reference to the theoretical hypothesis of a nationwide electoral district but it has never been set out in law.

The duration of their mandate coincides with the duration of the legislature, which in turn spans four annual legislative sessions (Article 153 of the CRP).

176. The selection of deputies to the Assembly of the Republic is carried out by universal, personal, secret and regular suffrage, according to the method of proportional representation using the d'Hondt system.

But the use of this specific method of converting votes into seats must take into account the prohibition to adopt barrier clauses: the electoral law 'shall not set down restrictions to the conversion of votes into seats by requiring a minimum percentage of the national vote' (Article 152(1) of the CRP).

Nominations of candidates to the election for the Assembly of the Republic are exclusively made by the political parties, either separately or in coalition (Article 151 of the CRP), although Portuguese Electoral Law has already proved to be open, at the local level, to independent candidates not supported by a political party.

177. The deputies, as members of the Assembly of the Republic, have functional situations, with a range of active and passive positions regulated by Constitutional Law:

- *powers relating to the exercise of parliamentary activity*, whereby they take part in the operation of the organ, and instrumental powers that enable the exercise of said powers;
- *rights relating to the benefits they are entitled to*, including remunerations and other material benefits;
- *immunities relating to the safeguard of the freedom to exercise their functions*, immunities which are divided into irresponsibility with regard to the opinions they issue and inviolability of their persons against the application of penal measures with various exceptions; and
- *duties relating to the proper performance of their parliamentary functions*, thus contributing to its maximum effectiveness. They consist in the responsibility they hold for their parliamentary powers, as well as other obligations such as transparency or those that flow from incompatibilities and incapacities.

178. The Assembly of the Republic is possibly the most complex organ the Theory of Constitutional Law is faced with. It is split up into various centres of decision-making that produce a politically meaningful will imputable to the State power.

The main decision-making centre of the Assembly of the Republic, which is also its ultimate decision-making centre, is the entire universe of its members, currently

230 deputies, gathered in the plenary assembly in which the essential powers of Parliament are vested.

However, the Assembly of the Republic also makes other important decisions, albeit not as relevant, within other decision-making centres (Article 175 of the CRP):

- *the Standing Committee of the Assembly of the Republic* – an organ which operates in the absence or inability of the plenary and guarantees the minimum vital functions of a democratic Parliament, among which are to be counted authorizing the President of the Republic to leave temporarily national territory and declaring a state of exception or a state of war, as well as general powers of political scrutiny and supervision and to ensure compliance with the Constitution;
- *the Chair of the Assembly of the Republic* – the organ responsible for conducting and administratively coordinating the parliamentary proceedings. It consists of a president (who is the President of the Assembly of the Republic), four vice presidents, four secretaries and four vice-secretaries, although in plenary sessions only the president and the secretaries sit in the chair;
- *specialized parliamentary committees* – organs that bring together several deputies according to their general parliamentary representation on the grounds of specific matters to be dealt with, permanently or for a limited period, the latter being the case of ad hoc parliamentary committees. Parliamentary committees of inquiry also belong here;
- *political groups* – organs that presuppose that their members hold special ties to the party which was at the root of their election to Parliament. They hold specific parliamentary powers, such as those of initiating legislation, tabling business or speaking during proceedings; and
- *the deputies* – organs that can act without having to be included in any other structure and for whom the CRP has expressly provided a regime of functional situations.

179. The proceedings of the Assembly of the Republic are of a permanent nature, for, in light of its prominent position in our representative democracy, it would be difficult to understand if it only worked intermittently or even temporarily.

The rules of procedure of the assembly are laid down in the Constitution – this also helps to prevent any attempt at restricting its political action. The proceedings correspond to the periods when the assembly is in session and their duration is annual, starting on 15 September and ending on 14 September of the following year, the period between 15 June and the end of the session being considered summer recess, without prejudice to the proceedings being prolonged, a fact that is almost inevitable in practice.

180. The powers of the Assembly of the Republic, allotted according to the various decision-making centres, are quite varied:

- *constitutional power*: to pass laws amending the Constitution;
- *political power*: to approve international treaties and agreements, and to produce acts of political scrutiny with regard to the government and to the administration in general; and
- *lawmaking power*: to enact laws and similar acts.

It has been debated whether the Assembly of the Republic is not also empowered to carry out administrative functions or jurisdictional functions. In the latter case, there is no doubt as to its impossibility; in the first case, the eventuality should not be immediately discarded, since the merely formal approval of laws is possible.

§3. The Government

181. The *Government* is the third organ of cabinet and it is a collegial organ, of a governing type, described by the CRP as 'the organ that conducts national affairs and the superior organ of public administration' (Article 182 of the CRP).

The status of the government is basically contained in the provisions of Section IV of Part III of the CRP, which is divided into three chapters:

(1) Chapter I – Function and Structure.
(2) Chapter II – Formation and Responsibility.
(3) Chapter III – Powers.

In addition two other laws should be noted, which lay down relevant provisions re garding the government's organization and workings, the Portuguese Government Organic Law (LOG) and the Portuguese Council of Ministers' Rules of Order (RCM).

The LOG defines the organizing structure of the government insofar as it has not been set out at the Constitutional level. It contains four chapters:

(1) Chapter I – *Structure of the Government.*
(2) Chapter II – *Powers of the Government Members.*
(3) Chapter III – *Organization of the Government.*
(4) Chapter IV – *Final and Transitory Provisions.*

To the RCM has been assigned a task mainly connected with the operation of the government and, in addition, the governmental lawmaking process and related activities. It contains five chapters:

(1) Chapter I – *Council of Ministers.*
(2) Chapter II – *Meetings of the Secretaries of State.*
(3) Chapter III – *Law-making procedure.*
(4) Chapter IV – *Other procedures.*
(5) Chapter V – *Final Provision.*

182. From the Constitutional perspective, the government consists of members holding various offices that are either *necessary*, or may be, in some cases, *eventual* (Article 183 of the CRP):

- the *necessary* offices – the prime minister, who is the Head of Government, the ministers, the secretaries of State and the undersecretaries of State; and
- the *eventual* offices: the vice-prime ministers.

From a legal viewpoint, the LOG lays down the composition of each government, within the Constitutional parameters. The Government 'comprises the Prime Minister, the Ministers, the Secretaries of State and Undersecretaries of State' (Article 185(1) of the CRP).

Under the LOG's pertinent provision, the prime minister shall be replaced, in his/her absence or inability to act, by the Minister of State and Foreign Affairs, or by another minister who is not absent or unable to act, according to the ministers' order of precedence within the Government.

The Government rests on a principle of collegiality that is emphasized in the Constitutional text in a peculiar manner, when it states in a provision dealing with government solidarity that 'the Government's programme and the decisions taken in the Council of Ministers are binding on the government members' (Article 189 of the CRP).

The Government's collegiality does not obliterate the functional predominance of the prime minister, to whom all the other members of the Government are answerable (Article 191 of the CRP).

183. The formation of the Government derives from the electoral results, which are reflected in the formation of majorities in the Assembly of the Republic, in view of the fact that 'The Prime Minister shall be appointed by the President of the Republic, after consultations with the parties represented in the Assembly of the Republic and with due consideration for the electoral results' (Article 187(1) of the CRP); these results are presumed to be the results of the elections to the Assembly of the Republic.

The President of the Republic appoints the other members of the Government on the recommendation of the prime minister; the same procedure applies to their removal from office (Article 187(2) of the CRP).

The term of office of the members of the Government, in contrast to the presidential and the parliamentary mandates, is not pre-established; it depends on the circumstances surrounding the appointment of a new Government.

The Government, collectively or individually, assumes office when it has been appointed and sworn in.

The Government ceases to hold office, also collectively or individually, according to three possible scenarios:

(1) *prime minister*: the moment he/she is removed from office; the new prime minister is immediately sworn in;
(2) *ministers*: the moment they are removed from office, or when the prime minister is removed from office, since this fact automatically implies that the ministers are also removed; and
(3) *secretaries and undersecretaries of State*: the moment they are removed from office, or when the prime minister and the ministers are removed from office, since this fact automatically implies that the secretaries and undersecretaries of State are also removed.

Contrary to an often expressed view, the resignation or the dismissal of the government, by itself alone, does not cause the cessation of office, either collectively or individually. They merely emerge from the Constitutional rationale of the CRP as a devitalizing factor in the government's political activity resulting in a caretaker government. The resignation or dismissal occurs in the following cases:

- *at the beginning of a new legislature*: the transition to a new legislature, due to the political accountability of the Government *vis-à-vis* the Assembly of the Republic, necessarily has to entail the resignation of the Government, thus allowing for the formation of a new government in accordance with the new composition of the assembly;
- *when the Head of State accepts the resignation* handed in by the prime minister: in view of the political and personal character of the Government and of the pre-eminence of the prime minister, the latter's wish to resign can only lead to such a result; this in spite of the fact that the resignation – with due consideration to the mission embraced when the Government presented its programme of action to the assembly and did not receive a vote of non-confidence – does not have to be accepted obligatorily where there are no relevant reasons for doing so;
- *when the prime minister dies or has a long-term physical incapacity*: here once again the importance of the prime minister in the functional dynamics of the Government implies this drastic consequence; it should be noted that the incapacity has to be lasting but not necessarily permanent and that it can be psychological;
- *when the Government's programme is rejected*, the non-approval of a confidence motion and the passing of a censure motion by the absolute majority of deputies present and entitled to vote: in all the preceding cases, the crucial relevance of the Government's accountability to the Assembly of the Republic becomes apparent; and
- *when the disruption of the proper working of the democratic institutions* occurs: this hypothesis is a security valve in the hands of the Head of State; it does not entail, at least literally, the existence of a mechanism of political responsibility, solely of institutional responsibility.

184. The Constitutional status of the Government with regard to the powers it holds contains clear provisions with regard to their three basic powers, which are:

(1) lawmaking powers;
(2) political powers; and
(3) administrative powers.

The lawmaking powers imply that the Government is, within the terms of the Constitution, a lawmaking organ, as the Assembly of the Republic is, although the powers of the first are exercised in less crucial sectors; the Government issues the corresponding decree-laws, which are within the parameters of its exclusive responsibility in the fields of organization and operation.

Political powers relate to the performance of a large number of acts concerning the relations with other organs of Government, such as the request that national referendums be called and the right of legislative initiative, in addition to acts related to the initial stages of the State's international negotiations with a view to concluding agreements and to the approval of international treaties within its powers.

The administrative powers are the most intense of the three insofar as the Government is in the eyes of the CRP the superior body of public administration; empowered to submit and execute the State plans and budget, enact the regulations aimed at the enforcement of laws, direct the departments and the activities of the direct central administration, oversee the indirect public administration and supervise the autonomous administration, perform duties related to civil servants and agents, besides upholding democratic legality and carrying out 'all the acts and laying down all the provisions that may prove necessary for the enhancement of economic and social development and the satisfaction of collective needs' (Article 199(g) of the CRP).

185. In a similar way to the Assembly of the Republic, the government has a mixed type of functioning at the level of various sub-organs, which are entitled to exercise some of the above-mentioned powers as provided for by the CRP or ordinary law.

The main structure of the government is *the Council of Ministers*, which consists of the prime minister and the ministers and in whom are vested the basic powers, such as the legislative and the political powers, namely the drawing of the general lines of government policy, the passage of decree-laws and the approval of international treaties, the approval of the plans and actions of the Government which may involve the increase or decrease of receipts or public expenses, to which must be added the residual power it holds since it can also decide on 'other matters within the government's powers entrusted to it by law or submitted by the Prime Minister or any other Minister' (Article 200(1)(g) of the CRP).

186. The Government may also act under other auspices, for instance, through sub-organs such as:

- The prime minister who conducts the general policy of the Government, coordinates and guides the actions of the ministers, directs the operations of the Government and its relationship with other organs of Government, keeps the Head of State informed about all matters relating to the conduct of internal and external affairs, has furthermore powers of his/her own and powers delegated by the Council of Ministers.
- The ministers who execute the Government's general policy with regard to their ministries, ensure, within the scope of their ministries, relations of a general character between the government and the other organs of Government, hold the powers that the Council of Ministers or the prime minister may have delegated to them, besides administrative powers of their own.
- The secretaries of State and the undersecretaries of State who do not hold powers of their own, except within the scope of their offices, and exercise the administrative powers delegated to them by the prime minister and their respective ministers.

187. The operation of the Government may also be considered from two further perspectives according to the extension of its powers:

(1) The *Government in full operation*: this is the usual situation where the government has the normal means to act and is duly legitimized by the assembly.

(2) The *Caretaker Government*: after dismissal or resignation and after being appointed, while waiting for the Assembly of the Republic to discuss its programme, 'the Government shall restrict its action to the acts that are strictly necessary in order to continue to address the business of government and ordinary matters of administration' (Article 186(5) of the CRP).

§4. Courts of Law

188. According to the CRP, the 'courts are the organs of government empowered with the administration of justice on behalf of the people' (Article 202(1) of the CRP).

It follows that the administration of justice is the sole responsibility of the *courts*, these appearing as a specific area in the organization of the constitutionally relevant public power.

The Constitution's concern with the courts is so great that it dedicates the whole of Section V of Part III of the CRP to the topic, albeit addressing also other matters that transcend the judiciary in its four chapters:

(1) Chapter I – *General Principles.*
(2) Chapter II – *Organization of the Judiciary.*
(3) Chapter III – *Status of the Judges.*
(4) Chapter IV – *Public Prosecution.*

189. It should also be noted that the CRP leaves the door open to a non-jurisdictional dispute resolution system by hinting that there may be non-jurisdictional instances invested with that power: the arbitral tribunals.

Arbitral tribunals are structures aimed at the resolution of disputes, which despite not being part of the formal judiciary, exercise powers delegated by the latter and are grounded in a voluntary choice with regard to either their judges – the arbitrators – or the submission of disputes to their judgment.

Arbitral tribunals may take one of two general forms, depending on the scheme under which they are formed:

(1) *voluntary arbitral tribunals and obligatory arbitral tribunals*: depending on whether they are chosen by the parties or their formation is imposed by law; and
(2) *ad hoc arbitral tribunals and permanent arbitral tribunals*: depending on whether the arbitrators are appointed specifically by reason of the dispute or their appointment is indefinite.

190. The organization of the courts is very complex in light of the multiple possible criteria for determining their jurisdictional powers. Faced with the evidence that the entirety of jurisdictional power cannot be concentrated in one single court, one must accept the inevitability of their proliferation.

That plurality of courts may be grouped according to two main criteria: the criterion of *hierarchy* and that of the *subject matter*.

The Constitution refers simultaneously to the two above-mentioned criteria when constructing the edifice of the Portuguese judiciary. There are, however, other important criteria to consider when ascertaining the powers of the courts.

191. From a material perspective, we are faced with the following set of materially distinct jurisdictions:

- *the Constitutional jurisdiction*– the Constitutional Court, which applies Constitutional Law. The CRP refers to it when it says that the 'Constitutional Court is the court specifically empowered to administer justice in matters related to the Constitution and the law' (Article 221 of the CRP);
- *the financial jurisdiction*– the Audit Court, which is 'the supreme body that reviews the legality of public expenditures and audits the accounts that must be submitted to it by law' (Article 214(1) of the CRP);
- *the administrative and fiscal jurisdiction* – the administrative and fiscal tribunals, which apply the administrative law and the tax law. The CRP refers to them saying that 'it is the responsibility of the administrative and fiscal tribunals to adjudicate the administrative cases and appeals seeking decisions on disputes arising from administrative and fiscal legal relations' (Article 212(3) of the CRP);
- *the civil and criminal jurisdiction* – the civil and criminal courts, which apply directly the other branches of the law, that is, civil law and criminal law. The CRP asserts that 'The courts of law are the courts with general jurisdiction in civil and criminal matters and in all other matters not assigned to other jurisdictions' (Article 211(1) of the CRP); and
- *other jurisdictions* – such as the maritime courts and the justices of peace, or the courts martial, which, however, only enjoy autonomy in a state of war, having 'jurisdiction to judge crimes of a strictly military nature' (Article 213 of the CRP).

192. From a hierarchical perspective, different situations may be observed, ranging from no differentiation at all to maximum structural differentiation:

- *one sole jurisdiction*, albeit with procedural mechanisms that permit more that one level of judicial decision, as, for instance, the Constitutional Court and the Court of Audit; and
- *differentiated jurisdictions*, where the courts appear divided into different categories, as is the case of the civil and criminal courts of law (district courts, courts of appeal and the Supreme Court of Justice), or of the administrative and fiscal tribunals (the administrative and fiscal tribunals, the central administrative tribunals of the North and of the South, the taxation tribunals and the Supreme Administrative Court).

193. The powers of the courts and of the other structures that may be connected with them are contained in the jurisdictional function of which they are the trusted guardians.

It is in the notion of 'administration of justice' that the meaning of the jurisdictional function is revealed: 'In the administration of justice the courts are under a duty to safeguard the rights and interests of citizens that are legally protected, to punish breaches of democratic legality and to resolve public and private disputes' (Article 202(2) of the CRP).

The jurisdictional function reflects the action of applying the law to cases arising from real life and it confers on the Court and other judicial instances the power to utter the definitive word with regard to the disputes they are called upon to settle.

194. On account of its relevance in the operation of justice, the status of the judges is dealt with extensively in the CRP. It is based on the following principles:

- *the principle of the unity of the magistrates' careers*: no interruption in their continuity or in the manner in which they are administratively managed is conceivable;
- *the principle of the independence of the magistrates*: 'The courts are independent and subject only to the law' (Article 203 of the CRP);
- *the principle of their irremovability from office*: 'The judges are irremovable and may not be transferred, suspended, sent into retirement or removed from office except as provided by law' (Article 216(1) of the CRP); and
- *the principle of irresponsibility*: 'The judges may not be held accountable for their decisions, except as provided by law' (Article 216 (2) of the CRP).

The judges are subject to various active and passive functional circumstances:

- *active* – the various rights to which they are entitled, from their salary to the guarantees regarding inviolability; and
- *passive* – the set of duties to which they are subject, well evidenced in the inhibition to perform other functions or to exercise political activities. In this respect it should be underlined that 'judges in office may not hold other public or private offices, with the exception of the performance of non-remunerated teaching or research duties related to legal matters, as provided by law' (Article 26(3) of the CRP).

The management of the judges' careers, likewise their deployment, is the responsibility of the Superior Council for the judiciary (*Conselho Superior da Magistratura*) that holds the following competences:

- *representative competences*: to represent the judiciary before other entities and, chiefly, before the government;
- *administrative competences*: in the deployment of judges and in their assessment and professional promotion; and
- *disciplinary competences*: in the application of disciplinary power in cases of disciplinary liability.

§5. The Constitutional Court

195. The Constitutional Court is unique among the various courts enshrined in the Constitution, in that there is a section dedicated to it. Its prominence at both the institutional and the ceremonial level stems from that fact, although the same conclusion may obviously be reached when one considers the relevance of its functions: to be the *supreme and ultimate guardian of the Constitution.*

The status of the Constitutional Court is further handled in important extra-constitutional provisions most of them included in the LTC, a legislative act with 115 articles, organized in sections:

- Section I – *General Provisions.*
- Section II – *Competence, Organization and Operation.*
- Section III – *Procedure.*
- Section IV – *Final and Transitory Provisions.*

196. The composition of the Constitutional Court comprises thirteen judges, occupying the post of councillor judges (*juízes conselheiros*), who hold office for a nine-year term, which is non-renewable even if it ceases beforehand on the grounds of resignation.

The judges of the Constitutional Court are appointed in two different manners:

(1) *By election*: ten judges are elected by the Assembly of the Republic by the favourable vote of two-thirds of the deputies voting, given that it is higher than the absolute majority of the deputies entitled to vote.
(2) *By co-option*: three judges are selected by their elected peers in a full session of the Court by an absolute majority vote.

The judges of this high court have the status inherent to councillor judges, the highest post in the career of judicial magistrates, with all the associated benefits and duties, and they are also entitled to carry a diplomatic passport.

197. According to the wording of the CRP, the Constitutional Court is generically: 'the Court entrusted with the administration of justice in matters relating to the Constitution or the law' (Article 221 of the CRP).

To describe in detail the Constitutional Court it is necessary to dissociate the various *specialized powers* it holds, the first of which is also much more relevant than all the others:

- *the power to adjudicate on Constitutional disputes*, it is this court that reviews the constitutionality of public law rules, representing the most critical power of this high court;
- *the power to adjudicate on disputes concerning reinforced legality*, relating to the infringement by other laws of laws with reinforced value;
- *the power to adjudicate on political disputes*, that is to intervene on disputes regarding the exercise of public office, such as that of President of the Republic and of deputy to the Assembly of the Republic;
- *the power to adjudicate on electoral disputes*, expressed in the review of the compliance with the law of the various elections;

- *the power to adjudicate on party-political disputes*, whereby the Court intervenes in the registration of parties and in the review of the compliance with the law of their internal elections and disciplinary procedures; and
- *the power to adjudicate on referendum disputes*, whereby the Court reviews matters connected with the proper implementation of the referendum procedures.

§6. Other Organs of Government

198. Having examined in detail the organs of Government, which are always Constitutional, we should complete our analysis by a reference to other government bodies, some of them also Constitutional, albeit not organs of government.

In most cases, the status of these organs pertains to various branches of the law, such as administrative law, law and economics and judiciary law, and is never exclusively defined by formal Constitutional Law.

The most significant of those bodies are mentioned below:

- *Mass Media Regulatory Authority (Entidade Reguladora da Comunicação Social)*: an independent body sponsored by the Assembly of the Republic; it has extensive powers in the field of mass media activities.
- *National Commission on Data Protection (Comissão Nacional de Protecção de Dados)*: an independent administrative body sponsored by the Assembly of the Republic; it performs functions to the effect of guaranteeing computerized personal data, and has powers of authorization and punishment to combat illegal activities; it consist of seven members, holding office for a five-year term.
- *Commission for Accessing Administrative Data (Comissão de Acesso a Dados Administrativos)*: 'an independent public body sponsored by the Assembly of the Republic'; it is responsible for promoting the implementation of the right of access to information held by public authorities (freedom of information).
- *Social and Economic Council (Conselho Económico e Social)*: it is an advisory body set out in the Economic Constitution, vested with the function of 'consultation and policy coordination in the field of economic and social policies, sharing in the framing of proposals for the main options and economic and social development plans and carrying out such functions as prescribed by law'.
- *National Elections Commission (Comissão Nacional de Eleições)*: a body of electoral management, distinct from the electoral judiciary organs (which are the courts of law) and independent; it may 'exercise its responsibility with regard to all the electoral registration procedures and elections to the organs of government, of the autonomous regions and of the local authorities'.
- There are two further bodies, which, on account of their significant role, deserve in this context to be more extensively analysed: *the Ombudsman (Provedor de Justiça)* and the *Council of State*.

199. The *Ombudsman* is located in the Constitution in his/her due place, as the protector of the rights of the citizens in a sense that extends beyond the mere upholding of the fundamental rights.

The Ombudsman is appointed by election, by the Assembly of the Republic, by the vote of a majority of two-thirds of the deputies, subject to the condition that it is higher than the absolute majority of the deputies entitled to vote. His/her term of office is four years, renewable once and he/she can appoint up to two adjunct ombudsmen.

The powers of the Ombudsman are essentially of recommendation: 'Citizens may submit complaints concerning acts or omissions on the part of public authorities to the Ombudsman, who shall undertake a review, without power of decision, and shall make such recommendations to the competent organs as are necessary to prevent or remedy injustice' (Article 23(1) of the CRP).

In some cases, however, his/her power may be of a binding nature, as occurs with accessing information since 'the services and agents of public administration shall cooperate with the Ombudsman in the discharge of his mission' (Article 23(4) of the CRP).

The Ombudsman heads various bureaucratic services – the Ombudsman's office (*Provedoria de Justiça*) – and is a public body 'independent from any non-judicial and judicial remedies provided in this Constitution and by law' (Article 23(2) of the CRP).

200. The *Council of State*, despite being an organ of the State, is not an organ of government; its status, from the viewpoint of Constitutional Law, is associated to that of the President of the Republic, the Council being defined as 'the political body that advises the President of the Republic' (Article 141 of the CRP).

The Council of State is a collegial body and its membership is justified on distinct grounds since it consists of the following:

- the President of the Republic who presides over it;
- the President of the Assembly of the Republic;
- the prime minister;
- the President of the Constitutional Court;
- the Ombudsman;
- the presidents of the regional governments;
- former presidents of the Republic elected under the present Constitution and who have not been removed from office;
- five citizens appointed by the President of the Republic for the duration of his/her term of office; and
- five citizens elected by the Assembly of the Republic according to the principle of proportional representation for the duration of the assembly.

The powers of the Council of State are *advisory* since the advisory opinions issued by it are not binding with regard to their conclusions. In some cases, however, its opinions are mandatorily issued, for instance on the dissolution of the national and regional legislative assemblies, the dismissal of the government, the declaration of a state of war and the making of peace, as well as the actions of the interim President of the Republic. Their absence may invalidate the final decision on those matters on procedural grounds.

With respect to the other issues, the advisory intervention of the Council of State, while not mandatory, may nevertheless be sought because the Council has the responsibility of 'advising in general the President of the Republic on the performance of his functions, whenever he seeks it' (Article 145(e) of the CRP).

The Council of State, being a collegial body, always meets in plenary sessions, convened by the Head of State, who also sets the order of business of the meetings.

Part III. The Portuguese State and Its Internal Organization

Chapter 1. The Fundamental Options in the Form of the Portuguese State

§1. Portugal as a Unitary State

201. From the many choices available regarding the definition of the form of State to be adopted in Portugal, the constituent lawmaker preferred the intermediate pattern of a *decentralized and unitary state.*

This is established in the initial provisions of the Constitution when it is stated that the 'State is unitary and complies in its structure and working with the autonomous system of the islands and the principles of subsidiarity, of local self-government and of the democratic decentralization of public administration' (Article 6(1) of the CRP).

In the paragraph that follows that first provision it is furthermore added that the 'archipelagos of the Azores and of Madeira shall constitute autonomous regions with their own political and administrative statutes and self-governing organs' (Article 6(2) of the CRP).

202. The unitary character of the Portuguese State, thus described at the internal level, *signifies the rejection of every kind of federalism; the constituent power, the power of constitutional amendment and the jurisdictional power remaining exclusive powers of the State.*

The above is easily understandable if one considers the small territorial size of Portugal and the absence of cultural, linguistic or religious asymmetries strong enough to justify an option for federalism.

The counter-proof of this lies in the absence of plurality in the elements that shape the State:

- there is only one Portuguese citizenship;
- public power is unitarily defined, and stems from a unique constituent power; and
- the territory is submitted exclusively to the power of the State.

§2. Portugal as a Decentralized, Regionalized, Communitarian and Lusophone State

203. Yet, symmetrically, the Constitution-makers were not tempted to go to the other extreme of conceiving the Portuguese State as the holder of all public powers. On the contrary, significant steps were taken – in particular in comparison with the situation before the Constitution of 1933 – towards implementing *political and legal decentralization*, as well as *administrative decentralization.*

The *political and legal decentralization* is a reality for the archipelagos of the Azores and Madeira, which constitute autonomous regions with extensive, political, legislative and administrative powers.

The *democratic and territorial administrative decentralization* is mainly reflected in the creation of minor public entities underpinned by people and a territory, which exercise administrative powers.

There are other modalities of administrative decentralization – such *as functional and associative decentralization* – which lead to the establishment of various types of public entities, all lacking a territorial basis.

204. The adequacy of the State's structure may also be analysed in its external dimension, for it is not feasible to conceive the State without placing it within the context of international society.

This would not be a particularly difficult task – it could be easily solved by asserting Portugal's external sovereignty as an independent power – were it not for the country's specific international ties by virtue of its membership of the European Community.

The fact is that since 1 January 1986 Portugal has been part of the UE, at the time the European Economic Community, and that membership is now reflected in the Constitutional text.

In the course of the Constitutional reform procedure that immediately followed Portugal's entry and took place in 1989, various provisions were set out aimed at adapting the Constitutional system to the requirements deriving from that entry:

- *on a programmatic level* – the assertion of Portuguese external policy as a policy aimed at European integration, as well as Portugal's contribution to its enhancement;
- *on a functional level* – the acceptance of the automatic incorporation of secondary community law sources, albeit without using the expression.

With the third Constitutional reform, the European clause of the CRP was strengthened, largely as a result of the planned ratification of the TUE, which was carried out in 1993.

The Constitutional reforms of 1997 and 2004 were similarly important from that perspective: the latter, for example, enshrined the primacy of European Union law over Portuguese law.

205. The European clause means that Portugal, despite maintaining the essential core of its sovereignty, suffers critical restrictions to it, insofar as the UE today is a supra-State entity with large amounts of public power that subordinates in many aspects the political power of the Member States.

This is why it can be rightly asserted that Portugal, like the other Member States of the UE, is a State with limited sovereignty or is an almost sovereign State.

206. However, the international projection of the Portuguese State is evidently not restricted to the principle of European integration. Many other policies guide Portugal's course in the international scene, which is more important than ever in our globalized world.

One of the other pillars of the Portuguese State's international presence is *Lusophone cooperation*, a consequence of Portugal's past ties with various Portuguese-speaking states, which thus rises to the position of being a fundamental vector of Portuguese international cooperation.

Chapter 2. The Political and Administrative Organization of the Archipelagos of the Azores and Madeira

§1. The Establishment of the Autonomous Regions of the Azores and of Madeira

207. Within the possible forms of organization of the State, the Portuguese Republic opted in the CRP for the unitary or simple State.

Yet the unity of the State contains within it the creation of *the autonomous regions of the Azores and of Madeira.* Nonetheless, however ample the regions' autonomy may be, they are still not endowed with the vital power of self-organization (*Kompetenz-Kompetenz*) since they wield no power that is independent from the power of the State.

The exercise of political power in Portugal, at the level of the political and legislative functions, is, therefore, split between the State and the autonomous regions.

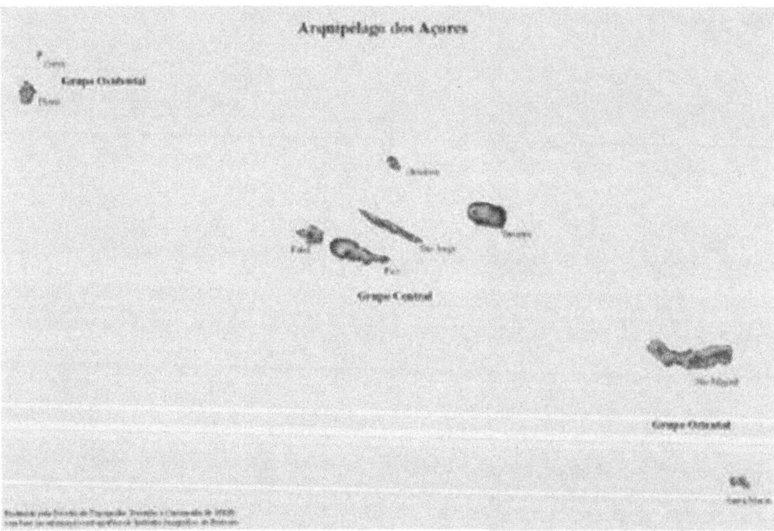

208. The legal status of these two corporate bodies rests essentially on the text of the CRP, which dedicates a whole section to them bearing a separate title: Section VII, with ten articles under the title 'Autonomous regions'.

Furthermore, their political and administrative statutes play an equally significant regulatory role. There is one for each region, framed in different periods, but offering, in practice, similar systematic and regulatory solutions for both entities.

209. The first definitive statutes to be approved were those of the Azores in 1980, containing 115 articles, thus distributed over its eight sections:

(1) Section I – *Azorian Autonomous Region.*
(2) Section II – *General Principles.*
(3) Section III – *Economic and Financial Provisions.*
(4) Section IV – *Regional Organs*
(5) Section V – *Relationship between Regional Organs and Other Public Authorities.*
(6) Section VI – *International Relations*
(7) Section VII – *Regional and State Administrations.*
(8) Section VIII – *Statutary Provisions Amendments.*

210. The statutes of Madeira were drafted much later, only in 1991, and are considerably longer, comprising 154 articles distributed over five sections:

(1) Section I – *Fundamental Principles.*
(2) Section II – *Organs of Self-government and Regional Public Administration.*
(3) Section III – *Relations between the State and the Region.*
(4) Section IV – *Of the Financial, Economic, and Fiscal System.*
(5) Section V – *Final Provisions.*

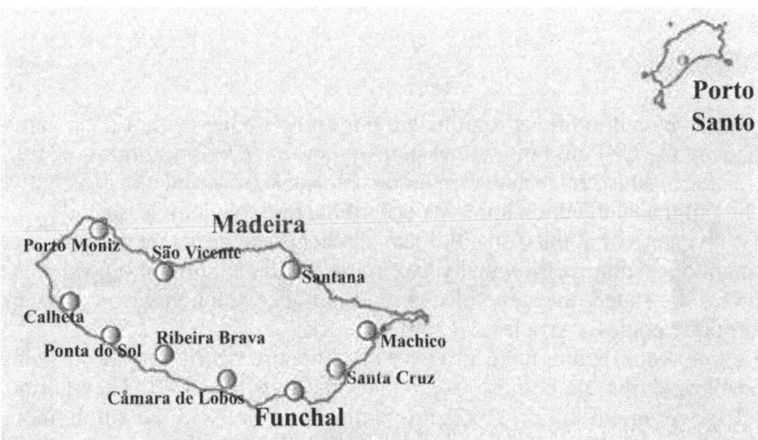

211. It must, nevertheless, be pointed out that the political and legislative regionalization of the archipelagos of the Azores and of Madeira cannot be said to constitute a total and heterogeneous phenomenon, notwithstanding the influences received first from Italy and, later, from Spain:

- *It is not total* because autonomous regions were only established in the two mentioned archipelagos, which appear to be the most important regions from the viewpoint of Portugal's geography, but are far from covering the whole Portuguese territory. Yet, at the same time, in light of their population profile and special characteristics, they seem to be the most deserving to participate in that political and legal phenomenon.

- *It is not heterogeneous* because regionalization is being implemented in the same manner in the two autonomous regions in what concerns its basic functional features – the dimension of their powers – and structural features – the organs and public services assigned to them.

212. The fact that the regionalization is political and legislative does not obviously entail the prohibition of a *parallel administrative regionalization*, insofar as the first certainly allows – or even imposes – the conferment of powers of an administrative nature.

As a consequence of their enshrinement in the Portuguese Constitutional system, the autonomous regions are vested with administrative powers, hence becoming new entities within the framework of Portuguese public administration.

Although it is our intention to focus on the political and legislative features of regionalization, it would be an oversight not to draw attention to that other dimension. The Constitution befuddles the issue by dealing separately, when defining decentralization from a public law perspective, with, on one side, the autonomous regions and, on the other, the local authorities – the latter in connection with other modalities of democratic decentralization of the public administration.

§2. The Regional Organs

213. Since the autonomous regions are corporate bodies with a legal status defined in part by the CRP and in another part by law, they possess organs of self-government, a crucial structural feature that our fundamental law considers a constitutive element of the political and administrative decentralization to be implemented.

It is not by chance that the Constitutional precept that appears on the title page of the CRP mentions with precision that very circumstance and, further on, when the pertinent powers are stated, the same idea is repeated 'The autonomous regions are territorial corporate bodies' (Article 227(1) of the CRP).

In the autonomous regions there also exist other organs, which, despite not being comprised in those corporate bodies, project unto them their actions. They are not organs of self-government but organs that operate exclusively in the autonomous regions: such is the case of the representatives of the Republic, one of which is appointed for each region.

214. Thus, in terms of organization, we should underline the existence of three organs that exercise their Constitutional and legal powers within the framework of the Portuguese autonomous regions:

(1) *The Legislative Assembly.*
(2) *The Regional Government.*
(3) *The Representative of the Republic.*

215. The *Legislative Assembly is an organ akin to a Parliament*; it represents all the Portuguese citizens resident in the region and the duration of its mandate is four years.

It is the only regional organ based on the universal and direct suffrage of the voters who reside in the regional territories. The conversion of the votes into seats follows the method of the highest average or d'Hondt system, a specific type of proportional representation.

The Legislative Assembly has the monopoly of the regional legislative power, as well as of the most important acts within the regional administrative functions and performs various political functions.

216. The *Regional Government is an organ of the executive type* entrusted with the conduct of the autonomous region's general policy in its various sectors and departments.

Its organization and functioning is set out under provisions of its own, for which the Regional Government is exclusively responsible. It is headed by a President and consists of regional secretaries responsible for the various sectors that are relevant to the Government of the Region.

The President of the Regional Government is appointed by the Representative of the Republic having regard to the electoral results. It is also up to the Representative of the Republic to appoint the regional secretaries on the recommendation of the President of the Regional Government.

The Regional Government holds, in addition to a range of administrative functions, powers of a political nature, both at the regional and at the national level.

217. The Representative of the Republic represents the State in the regional space; the structure of this organ is that of a single-member organ.

The President of the Republic, after seeking the opinion of the government, appoints and removes the representative from office. The duration of his/her term of office corresponds to the duration of the term of office of the president and he/she is replaced, in his/her absence and inabilities, by the President of the regional legislative assembly.

The Representative of the Republic holds necessary powers as provided under the CRP and eventual powers whenever the government so stipulates:

- The necessary powers are the powers of a political nature relating not only to the formation of the Regional Government but also to his/her participation in the regional lawmaking process, by way of the powers of signature and veto of regional laws.
- In the second case he/she may exercise, by delegation from the government, administrative powers of supervision over the departments and services of the State in the Region.

218. The regional system of government, in contrast with the national system of government, presents the distinctive feature of *being parliamentary*.

However, some necessary adaptations are required because the powers exercised by the regional organs must be combined with those exercised by the national organs.

Neither is it a semi-presidential system of government, for it is not possible to establish a double link of political accountability of the Regional Government simultaneously to the Legislative Assembly and to the Representative of the Republic. In reality, the political trust that must be expressed only works between the Regional Government and the Legislative Assembly, but not between the Regional Government and the Representative of the Republic.

It is true that the latter has the power to appoint the President of the Regional Government based on the regional electoral results, but it should not be inferred that there exists any kind of bond of political trust between the President of the Regional Government and the opinion that may be expressed by the Representative of the State.

219. Consequently, the pattern that better fits the organizational reality of the autonomous regions is that of *parliamentarism*, which can be of the assembly – when there is not a stable and homogeneous majority in the Legislative Assembly – or of the cabinet – when, by contrast, such majority exists. The centre of gravity of political action moves, in the second case, towards the Regional Government and its President.

The political practice that has developed over the past nearly twenty-five years of political and administrative regionalization in the islands – as a result of the more or less stable majorities that have been the norm there, to a greater degree in Madeira than in the Azores – emphasizes the *cabinet facet of this parliamentarism*.

§3. The Regional Powers

220. The most important of the regional powers is the *legislative power* translated in the production of *regional legislative decrees*, which are always enacted by the legislative assemblies.

The geographic reach of their application is restricted; it is confined, as may be expected, to the territorial limits of each of the archipelagos.

However, *existential limits* also affect this regional legislative power. They evoke the patent correlation with its own nature within the organization of the Portuguese Republic in its quality as a unitary State. The latter concept is a significant Constitutional principle with consequences even at the level of the material limits of Constitutional reform.

To the above we must add other *limits of a voluntary nature*, which the CRP chose to establish, counterbalancing in that way a certain intensity of the legislative autonomy conferred on the Portuguese autonomous regions amid many other possible options without prejudice to the principle of the unity of the State.

221. The sixth Constitutional reform, enacted in 2004, was going to modify the rationale behind the definition of the regional legislative power, bringing about a simplification and broadening thereof.

The regional lawmaking power expressed through the passage of the regional legislative decrees became subject, from the moment the amendments came into force, to a requirement somewhat less demanding than the specific regional interest: *that the autonomous regions be empowered to make law with regard to the whole set of matters that fall within their powers according to the design of the CRP and, above all, of their political and administrative statutes.*

With the disappearance of the provision concerning the 'specific regional interest', it no longer became necessary to prove in every case, with regard to a new provision, that it was prompted by a particular desire to forward the regional interest.

According to this new concept of the regional lawmaking power, it is the responsibility of the CRP and of each of the political and administrative statutes to define how far that legislative power can go. Indeed the CRP stipulates that the autonomous regions are entitled to 'legislate at the regional level in matters listed in the pertinent political and administrative statutes and that do not fall within the exclusive powers of the organs of government' (Article 227(1)(a) of the CRP).

222. At the level of the *negative requisites*, the presence of which prevents the regional lawmaking power from taking effect, only a few of the previous ones were kept. The duty for the regional laws to abide by the fundamental principles of the general laws of the Republic, for instance, was abolished. The notion simply disappeared. The following negative requisites remain:

- *the limitation of the Constitution and Constitutional matters*; the regional organs are always inhibited from legislating in their respect;
- *the limitation of the exclusive powers of lawmaking vested in the organs of government*, for those cases where the exercise of the regional legislative power is not admitted; and
- *the limitation of the partly exclusive lawmaking powers vested in the organs of government*, where regional legislative decrees are only permitted in case of delegation of that power by Parliament.

223. The combination of these different rules, applicable to the regional legislative function that is reserved to the legislative assemblies of the autonomous regions, results, when implementing the regional legislative autonomy, in solutions of a variable intensity. Three different hypotheses should be noted:

(1) *the primary legislative powers* – cases where the expression of the legislative power belongs solely to the regional Legislative Assembly; it is always a power in its own right and the possibility of inhibiting it at the national level is excluded;
(2) *delegated legislative powers* – cases where, by way of a law of delegation of the Assembly of the Republic, the regional Legislative Assembly is allowed to make law on such matters, being nonetheless compelled to obey the material guidance set out in the delegation; and
(3) *the legislative powers to regulate* – cases where it is permitted that the legislative assemblies lay down regulations to effect, with respect to the autonomous regions, the general legal bases contained in legislation passed at the national level, provided that the exercise of such complementary legislative power has not been reserved to the national organs.

Chapter 3. The Sub-State Administrative Organization

§1. Administrative Decentralization and the Administrative Function

224. It only makes sense to speak of public administration if one approaches the issue from the standpoint of administrative decentralization. This is the phenomenon that explains its most profound meaning, in a heterogeneous universe of entities contrasting private administration. By doing so, we shall be able to focus on the public administrative organization that takes root inside the State and respects its unitary sense.

The satisfaction of collective needs in an organized society cannot always be carried out by private initiative based on individual freedom.

There are multiple cases where it is not possible to do so without public power, either operating in parallel to private initiative, or even exclusively or predominantly with regard to the private sector.

And this is true for the most varied areas of human needs: from health to security, and from transport to justice, among others.

225. This is the reason why some of the individual or collective human needs cannot be entirely solved by private activity, and, in that context, the public power that shall satisfy them emerges.

Hence the *administrative function* arises, a function that is part of public power – alongside with the Constitutional function, the legislative function, the political function and the jurisdictional function – and is responsible for the satisfaction of the collective needs of individuals.

226. Three distinct but complementary dimensions may be observed in the context of administrative activity:

(1) *the administrative function of activity* – the satisfaction of the specific needs for security, culture and well-being;
(2) *the administrative function of organization* – the institutional structures to which the role of satisfying those needs is deferred; and
(3) *the administrative function of power* – the acts, which express the declarative and executive self-tutelage of law, which are produced by whoever may impose authority by contrast to private law grounded in the principles of liberty and equality.

§2. Entities of Portuguese Public Administration

227. The range of entities that perform the administrative function as described above are known as public administration and they contain the bodies corporate of a public law nature.

These are bodies corporate vested with powers of authority or *jus imperii*, which perform duties acknowledged by administrative law in the framework of the satisfaction of people's collective needs.

228. However, as a whole, they are all but homogeneous insofar as they can be of very diverse types. Taking as a reference the State administration, the following schemes may be noted:

- *the direct state administration*, which has the State as its highest legal entity, with regard to its attributions and its liberty to issue rules. It further possesses the power of direction that is the highest administrative power from the viewpoint of the direction of the administrative services and departments;
- *the indirect state administration*, which comprises the set of institutions that despite being formally autonomous in their existence and actions, are nevertheless bodies corporate in public law and address issues that may be ultimately identified as State interests and have been delegated by the State. As a result, these entities – public bodies and public corporations – pursue those interests in an autonomous manner and have intermediate powers of supervision over them; and
- *the state autonomous administration*, which comprises all those institutions that carry out functions of their own, separate from those of the State, and enjoy a larger autonomy with respect to the latter. The State only exercises a tenuous power of tutelage over such institutions that comprise public associations and independent administrative bodies.

229. Besides the above-mentioned bodies corporate that belong to administrative law, whatever the place they may occupy within it, we should equally identify the bodies corporate of public interest that, nevertheless, are not formally included in public administration.

On the contrary, on account of their functions and by virtue of some of the powers of authority vested in them, they are closely associated with public administration with which they maintain many connections.

Such institutions may be either akin to companies – *public interest companies* – or have another type of basis, related to patrimony or a particular individual – in this case they may be *bodies corporate for public benefit*.

§3. The Definition and Status of Local Authorities

230. The principle of the unity of the State not only contemplates the existence of autonomous regions but also coexists without difficulty with local authorities or other structures entrusted with public powers that are secondary in relation to the constituent power and the State legislative power.

Our purpose is to identify, among the large panoply of administrative power structures that permeates public administration, taken in the sense of a whole range of public legal entities, certain particular organizations vested with a larger administrative autonomy, significantly named 'local power'.

This is a further implementation of administrative decentralization, in this case of *territorial decentralization*, for it rests on the establishment of administrative entities based on a given territory and population, namely the local authorities.

231. Before providing a general description of the said authorities, we would like to point out that the administrative decentralization, which they embody, is quite distinct from the parallel phenomenon of *administrative de-concentration*, the name given to the transfer of powers to certain peripheral centres of decision, even though its direct connection with the action of local authorities may often justify a joint approach.

In order to distinguish the various types of de-concentrated administrative actions and avoid confusing the diverse powers, a division of the Portuguese administrative territory was necessary.

Hence the districts (*distritos*), an administrative division inherited from the preceding political system, have been maintained on a transitory basis, as stated in one of the transitory provisions of the CRP: 'Until the administrative regions are fully established, the areas not covered by them shall continue to be divided into districts' (Article 291(1), of the CRP).

The division into districts only applies to the continental territory. It has organs of its own, the civil governor (*governador civil*) and the district assembly (*assembleia distrital*). There are in total eighteen districts: Aveiro, Beja, Braga, Bragança, Castelo Branco, Coimbra, Évora, Faro, Guarda, Leiria, Lisboa, Portalegre, Porto, Santarém, Setúbal, Viana do Castelo, Vila Real e Viseu.

232. The legal status of local authorities appears autonomously in the Constitutional text, more precisely under Section VIII of Part III of the CRP that deals with 'Local government' and also mentions other bodies that cannot be assimilated to local authorities, such as the neighbourhood organizations, which do not meet the constitutive requirement of that concept.

Nevertheless, the most adequate characterization of the local authorities is to be found in the law, in particular in the Local Government Act (LAL), which sets out their organization and functioning in 104 provisions and 6 chapters:

(1) Chapter I – Object.
(2) Chapter II – Organs.
(3) Chapter III – Of the Parish (*freguesia*).
(4) Chapter IV – Of the Municipality (*município*).
(5) Chapter V – Common Provisions.
(6) Chapter VI – Final Provisions.

These numerous provisions address the large number of issues inevitably raised by the system of local government, such as:

- organic structure;
- local finances;
- powers and competences;
- creation, extinction and changes to boundaries;
- local referendum;

- administrative tutelage; and
- local authority employees.

Viana do Castelo
Braga
Bragança
Vila Real
Porto
Viseu
Aveiro
Guarda
Coimbra
Leiria
Castelo Branco
Santarém
Portalegre
Lisboa
Setúbal
Évora
Beja
Faro

233. Considering their importance, the Constitution provides a definition for local authorities, these being 'bodies corporate with representative organs serving the particular interests of the population in their territorial areas' (Article 235(2) of the CRP).

The above definition, freed from some imperfections it contains, points to the existence, in the concept of local authority, of four constitutive elements, that is:

(1) *the formal element*: an autonomous existence as a body corporate of a public law nature;
(2) *the human element*: the ties of the local authority to a set of citizens through the bond of residency in a dimension of democratic representation;
(3) *the territorial element*: the delimitation of the local authority's action according to a territorial dimension; and
(4) *the functional element*: powers and competences of an administrative nature, lesser in regard to the maximum power of the State.

§4. Types of Local Authorities

234. The form taken by local authorities under the above concept currently comprises two different modalities, since the administrative regions have not yet been duly established:

(1) the municipalities (also called *concelhos*); and
(2) the parishes (*freguesias*).

Three criteria provide a distinction between them: (i) the territorial size, (ii) the extent of powers and (iii) the structure of their organs.

The municipalities are fewer in number – 308 – and they usually encompass within their area more than one parish, whereas the parishes, with a smaller area, number 3,092 and correspond to the smallest and lowest administrative structure.

235. The reality of the Portuguese local government system, as set out in the CRP and by law, is not limited to these two types; other modalities of local organization are also admitted.

Such possibility is directly mentioned in the wording of the Constitution when it refers to the fact that 'For large urban areas and the islands, the law may establish other forms of local government that are appropriate to the particular local circumstances' (Article 236(3) of the CRP).

This means that, besides the fundamental structure of local government, the Constitution opens the door to the creation by ordinary law of special structures – which do not necessarily fit into the notion of local authority – for the purpose of solving specific problems, either of insularity, or of the great urban agglomerations.

236. When reviewing local organization in Portugal it is possible to observe various structures within the framework of the above-mentioned special local organization, which have become visible in law:

- the island councils (*conselhos de ilha*) – advisory organs created for the archipelago of the Azores;
- the metropolitan areas – either large metropolitan areas or urban communities; and
- neighbourhood organizations (*organizações de moradores*) – neighbourhood organizations 'of residents of areas smaller than their parish' (Article 263(1) of the CRP), which hold the right of 'petition before local authorities with regard to administrative matters of interest to the residents' and 'of participation, through their representatives, with no voting rights, in the parish assembly (*assembleia de freguesia*)' (Article 265 of the Constitution).

237. The Constitutional text also mentions the possibility for local authorities to join together with a view to pursuing common projects.

From the legal viewpoint, such hypothesis has become a reality both at the level of the municipalities – through *inter-municipal communities* – and of the parishes. Such associations may hold public law powers.

§5. The Structure of Local Authorities

238. The organizational structure of local authorities – that is, municipalities and parishes – rests on the duality: *deliberative organ versus executive organ*, reflecting the wish to endow each of these bodies corporate with instruments capable of expressing both of the foregoing relevant decisional levels.

Until the Constitutional reform of 1997, this was a constitutionally significant matter since the wording of the CRP laid down the foundations supporting the configuration of the organs of local government.

However, after the above-mentioned amendment of the Constitution came into force and in order to render the modification of their system easier, such modulation became, from that time on, dependent only on ordinary law with the additional requisite that the latter should be a law passed by two-thirds of the deputies to the Assembly of the Republic.

Since, up to the present time, no such law has yet been enacted and eight years have already gone by, the current organic structure is the one comprised in the LAL, that was passed in 1999.

239. The present Constitutional text, later complemented by ordinary law, addresses the opposition between:

- a *deliberative organ*, of a parliamentary type; and
- an *executive organ*, of a governing and collegial nature.

The *deliberative organ* consists of a larger number of members than the executive organ and it absorbs the most relevant powers, of a strategic nature, of the activities of the local authorities. This despite the fact that the *executive organ* – and, above all, its president – may stand out, inclusively on account of its more concrete character inherent to executive action. It is also held responsible to the deliberative organ.

240. Municipalities have as their organs the municipal assembly, the local authority executive (*câmara municipal*) and the mayor (*presidente da câmara municipal*).

The members of the above organs are directly elected by the citizens although less than half of the municipal assembly consists, ex officio, of the presidents of the parish councils (*presidentes de juntas de freguesia*) belonging to the area of the relevant municipality.

Parishes have as their organs the parish assembly and the parish council. The parish assembly is directly elected by the citizens registered in the corresponding area, whereas the parish council consists of members elected at the first meeting of the parish assembly; its president, however, is automatically the top-ranked candidate on the most voted list to the parish assembly.

241. The system of government that has been established for local authorities, that is, municipalities and parishes, has proven to be complex and, in particular, the source of many conflicts and inefficiencies.

This system, practically unchanged since its origin, peculiarly bears no direct connection to any of the best-known systems of government:

- *it is not parliamentary*, since the two executive organs are not politically responsible to the municipal assembly or to the parish assembly and these assemblies cannot be dissolved;
- *it is not presidential* because the executives are diarchic, this being more evident in the municipality than in the parish. In the case of the first there is a dissociation between the mayor, an organ by itself, and the municipal executive, despite the impossibility for the executive bodies to determine the dissolution of the municipal assembly, a power that is a fundamental feature of the presidential system; and
- *it is not semi-presidential* since neither the power of dissolution of the municipal assembly or of the parish assembly exists, and nor are the executive bodies politically responsible to their respective assembly.

242. It follows from the above process of elimination that the local government system should be described as *directorial*, in the manner of the French Constitution of 1795 or of the Swiss Constitution.

The foregoing description is the most adequate because it incorporates the notion of the separate existence of two organs for each of the powers at issue, without the possibility of reciprocal political responsibility: the restricted collegial body for the executive power and the parliamentary-type body for the deliberative power.

The touchstone of this characterization is the collegial feature of the executive body, which is not single in spite of being directly elected.

The problems connected with the present form of the local government system, in particular at the municipal level, are various and require an urgent reform.

Part IV. The Rights of the Citizens and the Safeguard of the Portuguese Constitution

Chapter 1. Fundamental Rights

§1. The Relevance of Fundamental Rights in Portugues Constitutional Law

243. The Constitutional protection of fundamental rights has been one of the more dynamic parts of Constitutional Law and has undergone far-reaching developments since the liberal revolutions. These started in the eighteenth century in the United States of America and in France and, throughout the nineteenth century, extended to other parts of the world, bringing with them the emergence of fundamental rights that have ever since been steadily growing in number.

This is why the Constitutional Law of a rule-of-law state, as contemporary political history can easily testify, cannot but pay careful attention to the protection of fundamental human rights, starting with the Constitutional texts and evolving therefrom.

Portugal, in that respect, is no exception – a fact that the evolution of its Constitutions, always echoing the various stages of recognition of fundamental rights, easily confirms.

244. In the nineteenth century, the first fundamental rights made their appearance in the Constitutional texts, closely linked to liberal political thought. They were either the subject of autonomous declarations or mentioned in the texts themselves, always according to the natural law theory largely developed by the Enlightenment philosophy.

This first generation of fundamental civil and political rights would, however, rapidly be joined by a second generation of fundamental social rights, dramatically claimed during the last quarter of the nineteenth century, at the time of the Social Question. The fundamental social rights protected the workers' and trade unions' interests and helped build the welfare state that would come fully into being in Europe after the Second World War.

More recently, since the sixties, a third and fourth generation of fundamental rights have emerged, which are not linked by a single guiding thread but give vent to new concerns related to multiple issues, such as the environment, the protection of the individual against its misuse, the protection of man against genetic manipulation or the right of peoples and nations to safeguard their cultural autonomy.

The evolution of Portuguese Constitutional Law partly reflects this itinerary, with the first four Constitutional texts – dating from 1822, 1826, 1838 and 1911 – showing a predominantly liberal view on fundamental rights. The Constitution of 1933, on the contrary, although drafted in the context of an authoritarian State, already enshrined some social rights. It was, however, only under the Constitution of 1976 that fundamental rights found their full effectiveness, in a global concept that covered all the generations of rights and freedoms having emerged in the course of the evolution of the contemporary State.

245. It should also be pointed out that Constitutional Law is definitely not the only branch of the law concerned with protecting the human being by way of the fundamental rights. On the contrary, this is an issue, which is dealt with transversally by various other branches.

Thus, for instance, at an early stage, civil law turned to the protection of personality rights. The first codifications, in the nineteenth century, already offered schemes of protection of an individual's privacy and personal inviolability. Such was the case in Portugal with the first Civil Code of 1867, a tradition followed again by the current Civil Code of 1966.

Likewise, in the twentieth century, Public International Law – followed in this by European Community Law – has seen the development of various systems of human rights protection, first at the universal level, within the framework of the United Nations Organization (ONU), but later continued at the regional level, in the Council of Europe, the organization of American states and the African Union. Portugal is fully bound by both the universal and the European systems of protection of human rights.

§2. Fundamental Rights in the Portuguese Constitution of 1976

246. In current Portuguese Constitutional Law, fundamental rights take a prominent place in Part I of the CRP. They are enshrined in a large number of articles, from Article 12 to Article 79, which means that most of them are enumerated and characterized.

Thus, in Part I of the Constitution, the listing of fundamental rights is divided into two separate groups: in Section II, 'Rights, freedoms and safeguards'; in Section III, 'Economic, social and cultural rights and duties'.

The difference between the two categories is not very clear, notwithstanding the variety of criteria that have been put forward in order to distinguish them, from the autonomous Constitutional density of the first, which is not found in the second, to their respective structures, of protection in the first case, of service in the second.

Whatever the case, and in the absence of a totally secure substantial criterion, the reason behind their dissociation lies in the differing legal force of each of them within the juridical order. Hence, rights and freedoms belong to the category of provisions with direct and immediate effect, while economic, social and cultural rights have a merely programmatic nature.

247. However, this does not mean that the Constitutional sources of fundamental rights are concentrated in the above-mentioned part of the Constitution, for it is possible to identify other sets of fundamental rights, that is, the non-enumerated fundamental rights:

- in Section I of Part I of the CRP, under 'General principles' of the 'Fundamental rights and duties';
- in Section I of Part II of the CRP, under 'General principles' of the 'Economic organization'; and
- in Section IX of Part III of the CRP, under 'Civil service', which is part of the general topic of the 'Organization of political power'.

248. It is also possible to find a few fundamental rights outside the Constitution. These acquire Constitutional force under the so-called open-end clause of Article 16(1) of the CRP, which states: 'Fundamental rights enshrined in the Constitution do not exclude any other fundamental rights contained in statutes or in applicable International Law rules.'

In this manner, the set of fundamental rights with Constitutional force becomes open to encompass other rights that have not been defined in the Constitution. The opening, however, is not indiscriminate since it is very judiciously linked to the following three parameters:

(1) the material breadth of the incorporated rights (their compatibility with the basic values of the Portuguese system of fundamental rights, the opening being thus neither total, nor neutral);
(2) the sources from which they stem (internal law and applicable international rules, this meaning that the rights must be preceded by a formal positivation); and
(3) the applicable regime (they share the same high protection granted by the Constitution's supremacy and the rigidity that goes with it; therefore, the notion that these rights might be secondary with regard to the fundamental rights asserted in the Constitutional text is not acceptable).

§3. The General System of Fundamental Rights

249. From the standpoint of a formal rationale, it is easy to explain that the fundamental rights proclaimed in the CRP are there because the Constitution-makers intended to bestow on them a formal recognition within a text endowed with the value of a Constitution, conferring on them in this way the highest legal force that a State's positive law can grant.

However, the legal and Constitutional positivation given to fundamental rights has another not less important reason, which also emphasizes their relevance: the fact that this positivation was accompanied by an autonomous definition and enumeration of the various types of fundamental rights.

Furthermore, on account of the mentioned open-end clause, the Constitutional catalogue of fundamental rights is at all times ready to incorporate further types of fundamental rights as a result of new needs or because corrections to the already existing must be introduced.

250. From the standpoint of a substantial rationale, fundamental rights enshrined in the Constitution are the composite outcome of various criteria that have been filtered by Constitutionalism over the years – from the liberal State to the welfare State. Nowadays, it is possible to say that there are several thematic poles around which fundamental rights gravitate and find their own explanation, based on a pluralist notion, on the influences to which they have been exposed and on their historical itinerary.

It is also interesting to note that the Portuguese Constitution is a good example of the harmonious composition of various existing trends with regard to the positivation of fundamental rights, namely:

- liberal fundamental rights, which are rooted in liberal theory. They present themselves as spaces of protection and autonomy *vis-à-vis* the State (rights and freedoms);
- social fundamental rights, imposed by social theory, for which such rights must be provided to the citizens by the State and other public bodies; and
- democratic fundamental rights, which pay tribute to democratic theory. According to the latter, certain rights play an important role in political participation by enabling citizens to be active players in political society.

251. In what concerns the rules that govern these fundamental rights in general, three issues should be addressed, other related questions appearing to be specific to the rights and freedoms and the economic, social and cultural rights.

First, subjective granting: the principle of universality implies that the holding of fundamental rights must be general, concerning every and all natural persons, whether national or non-national, with the exception of a few rights reserved to Portuguese citizens. Corporations may also hold fundamental rights if these are compatible with their structure; the principle of equality determines that fundamental rights must always abide by the rules dictated by the principle of equal treatment, both in its equalizing and its differentiating effects, discrimination being prohibited and some forms of positive discrimination accepted as long as they are materially founded.

Second, juridical exercise: the regulation of fundamental rights is conducted by Parliament. It gains thereby a higher standard of rationality and democracy. Any limitations laid down to their exercise are dictated solely by the need to protect other fundamental rights or Constitutional values worthy of protection.

Finally, effective protection: the protection of fundamental rights is broad. In its non-jurisdictional form, attention should be drawn to the growing role of the Ombudsman (*Provedor de Justiça*), while in its jurisdictional form it is provided by the courts that can invalidate unconstitutional legal provisions, as well as apply mechanisms of civil and criminal responsibility against the infringement of fundamental rights.

§4. Rights and Freedoms

252. The first part of the fundamental rights comprises the so-called rights and freedoms, consisting of three even more specific sets of rights, namely:

(1) *personal rights and freedoms*: those rights that relate to an individual's personal life; not only civil rights, but also rights pertaining to the enforcement of criminal law and of criminal procedural law;
(2) *rights and freedoms of political participation*: those rights that are connected to the intervention of Portuguese citizens in political decisions by way of elections, referenda or merely by shaping public opinion; and
(3) *workers' rights and freedoms*: those rights that concern the protection of workers' interests within the context of the enforcement of labour laws. They grant protection to the socially and economically weaker position of the worker in regard to the position of the employer.

The dividing line between each of the above sets of rights and freedoms does not always result very clear, but it is not far from the truth to say that each of them delimits a field of human activity, that is, personal life, political life and work life.

253. The specific relevance of the rights and freedoms can be basically assessed by the special legal force they carry in acknowledgement of the higher effectiveness of their enforcement, due not only to the fact that their commands become immediately operative, but also because they represent demands the citizen makes on the State and that can be immediately answered.

There is no doubt that the provisions governing the rights and freedoms apply to all fundamental rights recognized as such and placed in the Constitution under Section II of Part I since that is their function within the Constitutional organization.

However, the above conclusion should not be taken as exclusivist for the Constitutional text itself also places in the same system other fundamental rights, which it identifies as similar to the rights and freedoms.

254. In accordance with the contents of the rights and freedoms, their force in law is higher than that of economic, social and cultural rights, as is evident from the following characteristics:

- *Direct and immediate applicability*: the rights and freedoms, by virtue of the law under which they arise, are directly and immediately applicable in the legal order and do not depend upon the existence of favourable economic and social conditions. In addition, with very few exceptions, they are directly applicable without further enactment.
- *Binding effect on public and private bodies*: the rights and freedoms bind public bodies that are the emanation of the corresponding legislative, administrative and jurisdictional powers. In a smaller measure, they can also be applicable to legal relationships between private individuals depending on the degree of legal and social asymmetry that is present in them.
- *Limited possibility of being restricted under non-constitutional law*: the legislative is entitled to restrict the rights and freedoms but only to a very limited extent, limitations being both formal – provided for under the CRP – as well as material – the restrictions must be of a general and abstract nature, proportionate to achieve their legitimate ends, non-retroactive and shall never infringe the essential core of the rights.

– *Suspension in a state of exception*: the rights and freedoms may be suspended if a situation of Constitutional crisis arises during the states of siege and emergency in order that political and social upheaval may be countered. However, the suspension is always temporarily limited to a maximum of fifteen days at a time.

§5. Economic, Social and Cultural Rights

255. The other half that completes the global vision of the fundamental rights enshrined in the CRP concerns the economic, social and cultural rights, which, in turn, can be divided into three more specific sets of rights:

(1) *Economic rights and duties*: the rights that pertain to the organization of the economy, namely economic initiative and the rules governing private property, as well as the rights of consumers.
(2) *Social rights and duties*: the rights that concern the integration of citizens in the various social age groups, from childhood to old age, and that cover medical care, social security and housing.
(3) *Cultural rights and duties*: the rights that pertain to the instruction and education of individuals under which it is the State's duty to provide a public service of education at the various levels, to protect Portuguese culture and to further the practice of sports.

256. Compared with the rights and freedoms, the protection guaranteed by the economic, social and cultural rights is less intense from the point of view of the law due to the fact that they are enshrined in programmatic provisions and, as a result, cannot impose the same obligations of realization.

That trait is a general one. However, it also makes itself felt in various aspects of the specific regime that governs the above-mentioned rights, which certainly offers much less protection than the regime applicable to the right and freedoms, as can be seen from the following basic issues:

– *Indirect and mediate effect*: economic, social and cultural rights are not immediately enforceable; their fulfilment depends on the availability of favourable social and economic conditions.
– *Binding force on public bodies*: economic, social and cultural rights are not generically enforceable; they are essentially addressed at public authorities, binding them to the realization of the existing Constitutional programme on economic and social matters.

Chapter 2. The Guarantee of the Constitution and the Judicial Review of Constitutionality

§1. The Guarantee of the Constitution

257. The effectiveness of the Constitutional text demands that devices are laid down in order to guarantee its protection against unconstitutional acts, otherwise, the hierarchical supremacy of its provisions could not be upheld.

This is why the CRP establishes the general principle that all acts that violate any of the provisions and principles set out in it are void. Simultaneously, it lays down the general principle of civil liability for acts committed against the CRP.

However, there are also other specific defence mechanisms that seek to prevent specific unconstitutional situations, such as:

- The state of Constitutional exception: when the State, in response to institutional and political disturbances, suspends a certain number of rights and freedoms, and reinforces its administrative powers with a view to re-establishing Constitutional normality.
- The prohibition of fascist and racist associations: which is a case where freedom of association is not recognized on the grounds that these organizations infringe the fundamental values of the democratic Constitutional order.
- The right to resist, which consists in the possibility for citizens not to obey orders by public authorities that infringe their rights and freedoms, although as a subsidiary means and only when other legal means are unavailable.

§2. Constitutional Justice and Judicial Review of Constitutionality

258. However, the main defence mechanism of the CRP is judicial review, in particular the scrutiny conducted by the Constitutional Court.

The Constitutional Court is part of the judiciary together with the other tribunals. It comprises thirteen judges, ten elected by Parliament by a majority of two-thirds of its members and three who are co-opted by the elected judges, for a nine-year non-renewable term of office.

The result of a judicial review of constitutionality is a judicial judgment on the conformity with the CRP of all laws, procedures or actions by public bodies.

259. There are four different types of review:

- 'Preventive scrutiny' by the Constitutional Court, upon request of the President of the Republic, of the more relevant legislation. It takes place before the legislation is complete, since it is still awaiting the president's signature or promulgation.

- '*In concreto* review' conducted in a first stage by any ordinary court and, later, on appeal, by the Constitutional Court; it assesses the conformity with the Constitution of provisions applied in court decisions. Those that are ruled to be unconstitutional must be quashed and those that comply with the Constitution must be applied. This type of review may be initiated by the Court itself or upon request from one of the interested parties in the case.
- '*In abstracto* review', exclusively carried out by the Constitutional Court, assesses the conformity with the Constitution of legal provisions or actions by public bodies; should the Court decide that the provision is contrary to the Constitution, the unconstitutional provision is declared void and, therefore, it disappears from the juridical order with general effects. The ruling of the Constitutional Court is binding and has an *erga omnes* effect, even though there may be a few exceptions in the case of already-produced effects.
- 'Unconstitutionality by omission', this review is also exclusively carried out by the Constitutional Court. The Court verifies whether there has been a breach of the CRP, not on the grounds of acts contrary to its provisions, but as a result of the omission of enactment of legislative measures demanded by the Constitution. There is, therefore, a violation by inertia or failure to act, and in that case, the Constitutional Court is called upon to bring it to the knowledge of the concerned body in order that it may enact the missing legislative provisions.

260. The notion of Constitutional justice encompasses more than what has been described here. Indeed, the enforcement of the CRP is not restricted to the mechanism of judicial review.

Along with this scrutiny activity, there are other competences, most of which vested in the Constitutional Court, that are interesting from the standpoint of the enforcement of Constitutional Law:

- *electoral disputes*: the review of elections at their different stages from the moment that candidates are nominated to the proclamation of results;
- *institutional disputes*: the scrutiny of the exercise of public office, namely to ascertain the vacancy of the office of President of the Republic and the loss of parliamentary mandate of members of the Assembly of the Republic;
- *referenda disputes*: the *ex ante* review of the Constitutionality and legality of national, regional and local referendums; and
- *partisan disputes*: the review of the legality of elections and other ballots held within political parties, and of the establishment of parties.

Part V. Specific Issues of Portuguese Constitutional Law

Chapter 1. Constitutional Exception and Suspension of Fundamental Rights

§1. State of Siege and State of Emergency: State of War

261. The positivization of the state of exception in Portuguese Constitutional Law is grounded in the two notions of *state of siege* and of *state of emergency*: the first rooted in Portuguese Constitutionalism since it was first introduced by the 1911 Constitution and the second making its appearance in the CRP.

The connection between the state of Constitutional exception and the rights, freedoms and safeguards is quite obvious: the CRP only permits their suspension during a state of siege or a state of emergency on account of the purpose for which they are declared, the exception being strictly limited to the terms under which it can be exercised.

Hence, to study the suspension of the rights, freedoms and safeguards is also to study the state of exception in the CRP, albeit on a larger scale.

262. Portuguese Constitutional Law also lays down another device that is close to the state of Constitutional exception, namely the *state of war*. Although ignored by doctrine and scarcely developed from the legislative perspective, the concept is similarly relevant within the field of Public International Law.

Like the other two types of states of exception, the state of war is founded on various characteristic features:

- *the necessary preconditions*: under a military and more restricted viewpoint, the state of war is justified 'in the case of actual or imminent aggression' (Article 135(c) of the CRP) against the national territory;
- the *procedure*: the decision-making process leading to the declaration of a state of war implies the participation of the three politically active organs of government, the initiative falling within the powers of the government, the advice of the Council of State being subsequently sought before the intervention of the Assembly of the Republic, which authorizes it, and of the Head of State, who decrees it;

- the *effects*: since the CRP does not have much to say in that respect, merely providing the possibility of setting up courts martial, it is up to the Law of National Defence and of the Armed Forces to produce a densification of the deepest meaning of the state of war, which is to prepare the country to face the reality of war.

Notwithstanding the various points of contact between the state of war and the state of exception, apparent in the similarity of one of the necessary preconditions and in the homology of procedure, the two devices are distinct. The state of war is not endowed, as the state of exception is, with the potential to change substantially the Constitutional order – the only exception being that it permits the operation of courts martial, which do not function in times of peace. The CRP states: 'During a state of war, courts martial shall be established that have jurisdiction to hear crimes of a strictly military nature' (Article 213 of the CRP).

263. The Constitutional regime of the state of siege and of the state of emergency – which may be jointly named states of exception – was defined, in essence, at the outset, in the original version of the CRP. The subsequent Constitutional amendments were minor ones. In short, their contributions may be summarized as follows:

- *constitutional reform of 1982*– first, the increased democratization of the process of decision-making leading to the state of exception as a result of the heightened democracy achieved by the Portuguese system of government following the replacement of an organ of a military and revolutionary nature (the Council of Revolution). The intervention of the latter in the process – an authorization – was replaced by an intervention of an advisory type by the Council of State. Second a better safeguard obtained thanks to the increase in the number of expressly mentioned fundamental rights that could not be suspended in a state of exception; and
- *constitutional reform of 1989* – considerably less important than the first, this reform distinguished itself by a technical improvement of the rules governing the state of exception as a result of the clarification of doubts raised in doctrine by the initial wording, particularly with regard to the discipline of the formal legal aspects of the declaration of a state of exception.

264. The *normative sources* of the regulation of the state of exception, however, are not limited to the Constitutional text; both the international sources and the law sources should also be pointed out.

At the international level, Portugal is bound by the ONU and CEU systems of protection of human rights and, therefore, the pertinent texts are also applicable in this case.

And it should be underlined that, despite the fact that Portugal expressed some reservations in matters concerning the derogations to the rights of man set out in the International Covenant on Civil and Political Rights (PIDCP) and the CEDH, there is no evidence of any deviation from the provisions laid down, respectively, in their Articles 4 and 15, which are, therefore, fully applicable in the Portuguese legal order.

On the legal level, the Constitutional regime governing the state of exception is amply developed by a law dealing exclusively with these matters – the law on the regime of the state of siege and the state of emergency (LRESEE), the twenty-nine articles of which are comprised in the following chapters:

- Chapter I – *General Provisions.*
- Chapter II – *State of Siege and the State of Emergency.*
- Chapter III – *Declaration.*
- Chapter IV – *Execution of the Declaration.*
- Chapter V – *Procedure of Declaration.*

Notwithstanding its specific character, the foregoing law is not the only relevant one since there are others that handle at some point aspects of the regime governing the state of exception, for example, the legislation on the referendums, the legislation on the criminal responsibility of political office holders or the legislation on national defence and the armed forces.

§2. Fundamental Aspects of the Regime Governing the State of Exception

265. Once the normative sources of the regime governing the state of Constitutional exception have been described it becomes possible to deal with it along the following axes:

- the *necessary preconditions* – circumstances of political and social crisis;
- the *material effects* – the suspension of rights, freedoms and safeguards – and the organizational effects – a reinforcement of the administrative powers of the government;
- the *procedure for declaring* it – shared intervention of the politically active organs of government; and
- the *scrutiny of the execution* – entrusted to Parliament and the courts.

266. With regard to the necessary preconditions for declaring the state of exception, the Constitution sets out three possible sets of circumstances (see Article 19(2) of the CRP and Articles 1, 8 and 9 of the LRESEE):

(1) the 'actual or imminent aggression by foreign forces' – an event of an international military character whereby the territorial integrity of the State is harmed or is likely to be harmed;
(2) the 'serious threat to or disturbance of the democratic constitutional order' – an event of a political and institutional character, whereby the Constitutional structure of the State, in its core aspects and principles, is threatened;
(3) the 'public calamity' – an event of a social character, where there are considerable damages to a very large number of people caused by technological accidents or by natural disasters.

267. The *decision* to declare a state of exception – be it a state of siege or a state of emergency – is discretionary, delimited internally by one of the fundamental principles of public law, the principle of proportionality, under whose demanding terms the following effects are imposed:

- *the material effects* – the suspension of fundamental rights;
- *the organizational effects* – the taking of appropriate administrative measures;
- *the territorial effects* – the selection of which part of the national territory is to be affected by the declaration; and
- *the temporal effects* – the duration of the effects themselves.

The *material effects* comprise the suspension of the rights, freedoms and safeguards enshrined in the CRP. The LRESEE, however, stipulates restrictions on the rights that may be suspended.

The CRP, and subsequently the LRESEE, asserts also the impossibility of suspending the following fundamental rights: the rights to life, personal integrity and identity, civil capacity and citizenship, the non-retroactivity of criminal law, the defence rights of accused persons and the freedom of conscience and religion (Article 19(6) of the CRP).

The *organizational effects* are much more limited when compared to the material effects. In a general way, the reinforcement of the administrative powers of the government, the body responsible for the execution of the state of exception, is permitted: 'A declaration of a state of siege or a state of emergency shall vest the authorities with the powers to take the action necessary and appropriate for the prompt restoration of the constitutional normality' (Article 19(8) of the CRP).

The foregoing is explicable with reference to the traits inherent to the exercise of administrative power by the government; that is, its functional continuity, its restricted collegiality and the fact that it has control over the material means for the use of force – police and the armed forces.

In what concerns the non-administrative powers of the organs of government laid down in the Constitution, the general approach is to consider them untouchable and the same applies to the organs of the autonomous regions. The declaration of a state of exception does not imply any concentration of powers in the government. The latter merely sees its administrative powers reinforced, while the other organs continue to exercise their ordinary powers.

In certain cases, the state of exception may actually have the opposite effect of freezing the exercise of other Constitutional powers, which may not be exercised while it remains in force; thus, the dissolution of Parliament and the amendment of the Constitution are prohibited.

268. It should be noted, with regard to the declaration of a state of siege or a state of emergency, that a procedure is followed, which involves the various organs of government and clearly shows the extraordinary importance the CRP wished to confer on the state of Constitutional exception:

- The *initiative of the President of the Republic* – once the necessary preconditions have been fulfilled, the Head of State is responsible for initiating unofficially, by drafting a declaration, a procedure leading to the declaration of a state of siege and a state of emergency.

- The *consultation of the Government*, on an inquiry basis – in view of his/her intention to initiate the procedure, the President of the Republic must consult the government, which returns a mandatory but non-binding opinion.
- The *authorization of the Assembly of the Republic* – the draft declaration, duly accompanied by the government's advisory opinion, is subsequently laid before the Assembly of the Republic, which authorizes or does not authorize the declaration, but is barred from amending it.
- The *final decision of the President of the Republic* – if Parliament has given its authorization, the President of the Republic has the last say in the matter, declaring or not declaring the state of siege or emergency in the precise terms that have been proposed (and having regard to the need for the government's counter-signature).

269. The care with which the Constitutional lawmaker framed a regime for the state of exception that would comply with the demanding principles of the rule of law enshrined in the CRP is also patent in the type of scrutiny provided for its various actions.

The *political scrutiny* is entrusted to the Assembly of the Republic, which is responsible for reviewing *ex post* the execution of the state of exception by imposing political responsibility – through the passing of a motion of censure leading to the fall of the government – or criminal responsibility – by bringing charges via parliamentary scrutiny committees.

The *judicial review* is carried out almost exclusively by the Constitutional Court that is responsible for assessing the compliance with the Constitution of the acts of a normative nature connected with the declaration and execution of a state of exception. For their part, the other courts are responsible for reviewing the legality of the non-normative acts, as well as for imposing criminal and civil responsibility that may result from the practice of such acts.

Chapter 2. State and Religion

§1. The Importance of Religion to Man and Society

270. It is not necessary to go very far if one wishes to justify the importance of the religious phenomenon in human activity, something that even the most convinced atheist dares not deny.

From the anthropological standpoint, it is nowadays scientifically proven that *homo sapiens* coincided with the appearance of *homo religiosus* and, therefore, it is easy to understand that mankind goes hand in hand with religiosity.

This is why since primitive times and until current times the presence of religion – of any sort – has remained constant and, consequently, it is possible to affirm that religiosity is an integral part of mankind and that, symmetrically, without mankind there is no religiosity.

271. But if religiosity is an unequivocal attribute of mankind, considered individually, it is equally present at the level of the organization of society, in the relationships that are established between people within the context of the various groups they belong to.

This means that religion transcends the individual and reaches vast spheres of the collectivity in its most diverse manifestations, from the nuclear family to the international community, encompassing, on its way, the State itself.

Hence it is not too daring to assert that religion is also inherent to man's sociability and that the latter, in his inter-individual relationships, is similarly guided by criteria of a religious nature.

272. It is but a short step from the importance of religion in society to the necessity of its being regulated by law, given that it is the law's responsibility to lay down guidelines for the establishment of relationships between individuals and groups in each and every sphere of community life.

If religion is not restricted to the individual dimension and is also present in collective manifestations of human sociability, then the law, since its ultimate end is to secure justice and ensure security in social relations, has a regulatory role to play with regard to it. For that purpose it can count on the application of sanctions using a coercive political power that shall be at its service.

It is a fact that the law imbued in the social order is not always and necessarily assisted by such constraining protection. However, it is not less true that the Law of the State – which is the most reliable sector in the protection of human society organized under the form of a State – is the law better characterized by its power of coercion, which enables it to impose, by force if necessary, compliance with the law and to repress any breach thereof.

§2. The Evolution of Relations Between the State and Religion

273. Despite the fact that the State and the law nowadays deal with religion in a respectful manner, it is worthwhile to provide a brief description of the historical evolution of those relations. It should be noted, by the way, that the present status is the result of enormous efforts, of all kinds, being deployed and that there are still unsolved issues.

We shall naturally mention more frequently the Christian religion as it has accompanied the development of the State – fundamentally Eurocentric in Western culture – within which framework many of our present political and Constitutional institutions have seen the light of the day and grown.

Such predominance cannot signify, of course, that other religions, in some cases with higher numbers of adherents and in respect to which a growing interest and appreciation have lately arisen, should be ignored.

274. It is quite clear that, practically since the first beginnings of the State, religion has always played a central role along with other defining elements of the State.

For instance, in classical antiquity several experiences took place that showed a variety of possible relations between religion, the State and the law:

- In the Eastern State, up to the *apogée* of ancient Greece, there is a predominance of states originating directly in religion – theocratic monarchies – in the sense that the religious function was vested in the kings, sometimes adored as gods, as was the case in Mesopotamia, Egypt or Israel, although each with different specific characteristics.
- In the Greek and the Roman states, within their professed polytheistic religions, theocratic conceptions were also dominant, evolving, in the case of Rome, into the divinization of the emperor himself.

275. With the passage of time to the Middle Ages and the predominance of the Christian religion in Europe, political power and religious power gradually developed structures of their own and, consequently, they progressively became distinct. This, however, did not inhibit their mutual interference on the basis of two models that would succeed one another due to several historical and political factors:

(1) In a first phase, the Byzantine caesaro-papism, in the Eastern Roman Empire, with the dominance of the emperor over the Christian religion, he/she who would be the heir to the caesaro-papism of the Western Roman Empire in its last phase, when the Christian faith from being merely tolerated would become the official and regulated religion of the empire.
(2) In a second phase, the mediaeval hierocratism, where notwithstanding the claims of the theory of the two swords – temporal power and spiritual power – in the relationship between the State and the Church, the standpoint of the spiritual power would prevail at the end.

276. In the Modern Age, born with the Renaissance and the discoveries, and intent on the rediscovery of classical humanism, the religious division of Europe takes place, and the religions become State religions, thus paving the way for the State, since it has an official religion, to make laws of a religious nature.

Simultaneously this was also going to be, in Europe, a period of growing assertion of the sovereign power of the State itself, which would lead to absolute royal power, in which the Christian religious faiths, in their various divisions, would play an important role as a political element of a new concept of State power.

§3. The Predominance of the Model of Republican Secularism

277. Only in the Contemporary Age did the foundations of secularism, where there is separation between State and Churches, or generically speaking between the law and religion, take root.

Yet this period is far from linear since several distinct experiences run through it:

- the experience of North-American secularism where the State, in a climate of religious pluralism, sociologically induced by the diversity existing in the former colonies of North America, collaborates with the religions and recognizes and accepts them in the public space;
- the experience of French secularism where the State assumes the role of the 'enemy' of religion, bent on suppressing its traces, in a fight that is essentially political against the dominant religion, the Catholic Church; and
- the experience of soviet secularism where the State persecutes religion as an 'obscurantist' manifestation – 'the opium of the people', in the words of Karl Marx – and considers it an ally of the bourgeoisie, obstructing the road to communist society and man.

278. Consequently, nowadays, the model of the separation between State and Churches, and also between the law and religion, is spreading, albeit according to different schemes:

- cooperative separation, where the State, pursuing identical aims, collaborates with religious faiths in activities undertaken by the latter; and
- neutral separation, where the State does not intervene in any activities jointly with religious faiths.

279. There are undeniable advantages in the model of separation between State and Churches since some principles and guidelines arise from it that are of benefit to all:

- the freedom of religion and conscience – if the State remains silent on the matter, then each individual and group is free to choose his/her religion, to practise it, to leave it and to join it again according to the criteria of each of the religions at issue;

- the principle of equality in the treatment of religions – if there is no official religion, then there are no unfavourable treatments but only the acknowledgement of a social and human reality with whom the State may collaborate for certain purposes; and
- the democratic principle insofar as the separation between State and religious faiths prevents the political power from becoming the prey of any religion, all party-political groups being allowed to gain and exercise political power regardless of their religious allegiance.

§4. The Evolution of the Relationship Between Portuguese Constitutionalism and Religion

280. It goes without saying that the formation and evolution of the Portuguese State could not but be sensitive to these fundamental vectors in the appearance of the various models of relationship between law and religion, in particular Roman Catholicism.

That presence was felt at the very moment of the birth of Portugal, in two distinct historical events:

(1) when the future first King, D. Afonso Henriques, after the Battle of Ourique in 1139, received a divine Christian revelation and gained the courage to fight the 'sarracens'; and
(2) when Pope Alexander III, in 1179, conferred the title of *rex* to that same D. Afonso Henrique by the Papal Bull *Manifestis probatum*.

Hence, during the entire pre-Constitutional period and with some rather unedifying episodes along the way, such as those which occurred at the time of the Marquês de Pombal, Portugal went from mediaeval hierocratism, first, with the Pope intervening in many internal affairs, such as the discovered territories and the Treaty of Tordesilhas, to, at a later time, after the advent of the absolutist State.

281. Curiously, during the first Constitutional age, in the nineteenth century, no significant changes arose from the Constitution of 1822, the Constitutional Charter of 1826 and the Constitution of 1838. The system continued to be one of official religion albeit with progressive but timid attempts at introducing some tolerance for other religions. Thus:

- in the Constitution of 1822, Article 19 stipulated as one of the duties of the Portuguese the need to 'venerate religion';
- in the Constitutional Charter of 1826, Article 6 established that 'All the other religions shall be permitted to foreigners, who shall be allowed to worship in their homes or in houses to that effect which shall not take the exterior form of a temple'; and
- in the Constitution of 1838, Article 3 asserts, 'The State's religion is the Roman Catholic and Apostolic Religion'.

282. The scene underwent a radical change when the Revolution of 5 October 1910 proclaimed the Republic and headed towards a secular model of religious persecution, the victim of which was to be the main religion; that is, the Catholic Church.

The Constitution of 1911 enshrined in its apparent simplicity a model of secularism, of neutral separation between State and religion, with its Article 3(4) and following laying down several provisions to that effect.

Yet the implementation of the significant Separation Act, enacted before the framing of the Constitution of 1911, was going to attest the actual presence of a model of true persecution against religion, aimed against the Catholic Church.

Political practice, as well as some ordinary laws passed at the time, pointed indeed in that direction: they joined in a frenzied attack against the Catholic Church, whose properties were confiscated and religious orders dissolved. The part that some radical freemason groups played in these attacks was decisive.

283. With the inauguration of the *Estado Novo* regime after the military coup of 28 May 1926, a new course was steered, that of reconciliation between the State and the Catholic Church. Formally the principle of secularism was applied, but in practice a more favourable treatment was accorded to the latter religion.

The principle of the separation between State and religious confessions was going to be enshrined in Article 46 of the Constitution of 1933 in the following terms: 'Without prejudice to the provisions of the concordats concerning the *Padroado* (patronage of missions), the State maintains the regime of separation with regard to the Catholic Church and any other religion or cults practised within the Portuguese territory.'

Yet this regime of separation coexisted with the particular treatment granted to the catholic faith, not only in practice but also as a result of the celebration of the Concordat of 1940, and not to mention the subsequent evolution of the wording of the Constitution, which, in the new Article 45 introduced by the Constitutional reform of 1951, defined the Catholic faith as 'the religion of the Portuguese Nation'.

284. In the wake of the 25 April 1974 Revolution, known as the Revolution of the Carnations and following the adoption of the Constitution of 2 April 1976, a new model emerged that kept to the line of separation between State and religious faiths, but where the first acknowledges and protects the latter.

On the plane of the fundamental rights, the freedom of conscience and religion, both from an individual and a collective viewpoint, is extensively dealt with and enshrined in this Constitution.

At the level of the organization of political power, the State is declared to be nonconfessional – the Portuguese State does not have a religion – and the separation between State and Churches is raised to the status of material limit of Constitutional reform.

§5. The Present Constitutional and Legal System of Cooperative Separation Between State and Religion

285. The other dimension that is similarly present in the republican principle embodied in Portuguese Constitutional Law corresponds to the application of the *model of cooperative separation* between political power and religious phenomenon.

This is a matter that is equally relevant from the standpoint of the CRP, which does not refrain from setting out various rules and principles in that respect:

- *at the level of the safeguarding of fundamental rights*, it asserts the freedom of religion and conscience with several tiers of protection (Article 41 of the CRP); and
- *at the level of the political organization*, this issue has been elevated to the rank of material limit of Constitutional reform (Article 288(c) of the CRP).

The sub-Constitutional legislation, on the contrary, has complemented the guidance drawn up by the Constitution with the Religious Freedom Act (LLR), as well as a large amount of complementary legislation generically applicable to all religions; furthermore, a new concordat between Portugal and the Holy See was signed on 18 May 2004.

286. In what concerns the fundamental rights, the core precept consists in the positivization of the *freedom of conscience and religion*; in its first paragraph it stipulates 'Freedom of conscience, religion and worship is inviolable' (Article 41(1) of the CRP).

This fundamental right irradiates from there to other specific spheres where the importance of religious activity is equally felt:

- on an *individual basis* through the free activity of people in the manifestation of their religious faith, either in private or in public, in worship or any other pertinent manifestation; and
- on an *institutional basis* through the free establishment of religious associations and their liberty of organization and activity that may benefit from the protection of the State and the legal order.

287. The organization of political power, for its part, is in accordance with the notion of separation between political power and religious phenomenon. Identification between or, even worse, fusion of these two spheres of collective life is impossible.

In various fields where it operates, the State is expected to be guided by *religious neutrality*:

- *in the media*: 'Freedom is guaranteed to each denomination to teach its religion and to use its own media to carry out pertinent activities' (Article 41(5) of the CRP);
- *in public education and culture*: 'The State shall not plan education and cultural development in accordance with any philosophical, aesthetic, political, ideological or religious precepts' (Article 43(2) of the CRP); and
- *in public education*: 'Public education shall be non-denominational' (Article 43(3) of the CRP).

And to confirm the foregoing, in addition to the principle of non-interference of religion with the organization of political powers, it is expressly stipulated with respect to the material limits of Constitutional reform 'The laws revising this Constitution shall respect: □ The separation of Churches and State' (Article 288(c) of the CRP).

288. A reading of the LLR confirms entirely everything we have said since it rests on two structuring principles of the model of cooperative separation between State, law and religion:

(1) on the one hand, the principle of separation. Article 3 asserts that 'The Churches and other religious communities are separated from the State and free in their organization and exercise of their functions and worship'; and
(2) on the other, the principle of cooperation, under which, as may be inferred from Article 5 of the mentioned law, 'The Portuguese State shall collaborate with the Churches and the religious communities based in Portugal having regard to their degree of representativity and in view namely of promoting human rights, enhancing the integral development of each individual person and fostering the values of peace, liberty, solidarity and tolerance'.

289. With regard to sub-Constitutional legislation, the enactment in 2001 of the LLR should be underlined. It updated the Religion Law in Portugal, revoking Law No. 4/71, which formerly provided guidance on the matter at issue.

The LLR consists of sixty-nine articles organized in the following eight chapters:

(1) Chapter I – *Principles.*
(2) Chapter II – *Individual Rights of Religious Freedom.*
(3) Chapter III – *Collective Rights of Religious Freedom.*
(4) Chapter IV – *Status of the Churches and Religious Communities.*
(5) Chapter V – *Agreements between Religious Bodies Corporate and the State.*
(6) Chapter VI – *Commission for Religious Freedom.*
(7) Chapter VII – *The Catholic Church.*
(8) Chapter VIII – *Complementary and Transitional Provisions.*

290. There are many relevant innovations to be underlined in this LLR that deserve high praise:

- the innovation in the employment status of workers who profess a religion, whereby the respective days of rest and worship are upheld;
- the acknowledgement of the civil effects, in general terms, of religious marriage;
- the institutionalized and organized acceptance of religious assistance attesting to a public interest in this matter on the part of the State; and
- the protection of the religious cultural goods and the town-planning concerns over the location of Church goods.

291. Finally, mention should be made of the important contribution of the Constitutional Court, which has been shaping, in many of its decisions, significant jurisprudential guidance.

Selected Bibliography

I. Constitutional Doctrine

Bacelar Gouveia, J. *Manual de Direito Constitucional*, 6th edn. I e II, Coimbra: Almedina, 2016; *Constitutional Law*, in AAVV. *Portuguese Law – An Overview*. Lisboa: Almedina, 2007, 75 e ss.; *Fundamental Rights*, in AAVV. *Portuguese Law – An Overview*. Lisboa: Almedina, 2007, 89 e ss.

Gomes Canotilho, J.J. *Direito Constitucional e Teoria da Constituição*. 7th edn. Coimbra: Almedina, 2003.

Gomes Canotilho, J.J. & V. Moreira. *Fundamentos da Constituição*. Coimbra: Coimbra Editora, 1988; *Constituição da República Portuguesa anotada*. 4th edn. Coimbra: Coimbra Editora, 1993.

Miranda, J. *A Constituição de 1976 – formação, estrutura e princípios fundamentais*. Lisboa: Livraria Petrony, 1978; *Manual de Direito Constitucional*, I, II, III, IV, V, VI e VII, Coimbra: Coimbra Editora, 2000 a 2007.

Rebelo de Sousa, M. *Direito Constitucional – Introdução à Teoria da Constituição*. Braga: Livraria Cruz, 1979.

II. Constitution and Other Fundamental Law – Texts

Bacelar Gouveia, J. Legislação de direitos fundamentais. 2nd edn. Coimbra: Almedina, 2005; As Constituições dos Estados de Língua Portuguesa. 3rd edn. Coimbra: Almedina, 2012; Legislação de Direito Constitucional. 3rd edn. Lisbon: Quid Juris, 2013.

Miranda, J. *Constituições Portuguesas*. 5th edn. Lisboa: Livraria Petrony, 2004.

Selected Bibliography

Index

The numbers here refer to paragraph numbers

Armed Forces, 20, 169, 262, 264, 267
Autonomous Regions, 13, 21, 22, 24, 25, 94, 106, 107, 109, 110, 111, 112, 113, 118, 126, 146, 162, 198, 201, 203, 207, 208, 211, 212, 213, 214, 219, 220, 221, 223, 230, 267

Citizenship, 6, 7, 8, 9, 156, 202, 268
Constituent power, 33, 46, 47, 48, 49, 50, 51, 52, 53, 54, 55, 56, 57, 62, 63, 64, 65, 74, 202, 230
Constitutional conventions, 79, 83
Constitutional custom, 69, 70, 71, 72
Constitutional jurisprudence, 75, 78, 147
Constitutional reform, 20, 49, 57, 58, 59, 60, 61, 62, 63, 64, 65, 66, 68, 74, 114, 146, 204, 220, 221, 263, 283, 284, 287
Constitutionalism, 3, 24, 41, 51, 90, 250, 261, 280

Democracy, 4, 20, 22, 74, 122, 124, 125, 127, 128, 129, 137, 142, 143, 145, 148, 155, 156, 157, 160, 163, 172, 179, 251, 263
Deputies, 116, 118, 151, 168, 174, 175, 176, 177, 178, 183, 196, 199, 238
Districts, 23, 154, 175, 231

Elections, 45, 96, 128, 130, 131, 132, 133, 137, 139, 142, 150, 155, 157, 166, 168, 170, 183, 197, 198, 252, 260
Electoral system, 134, 135, 136
Equity, 79, 82

Fundamental rights, 22, 45, 158, 160, 199, 243, 244, 245, 246, 247, 248, 249, 250, 252, 255, 263, 284, 286

Government, 9, 13, 21, 23, 26, 28, 60, 87, 89, 90, 95, 96, 104, 105, 106, 108, 110, 111, 112, 113, 116, 118, 120, 146, 149, 172, 179

International Law, 90, 91, 92, 245, 248, 262

Judicial review, 25, 151, 154, 167, 257, 258, 260, 269

Legislative acts, 23, 45, 86, 93, 94, 102, 103, 104, 105, 107, 108, 110, 111, 112, 113, 114, 117, 119
Legislative power, 21, 24, 25, 60, 90, 107, 108, 109, 113, 215, 220, 221, 222, 223, 230
Legislative process, 60, 118, 120
Local government, 13, 26, 126, 232, 235, 238, 242

Monarchy, 2
Municipality, 26, 232, 240, 241

Nationality, 9

Ombudsman, 198, 199, 200, 251
Ordinary laws, 7, 33, 147, 159, 185, 235, 238, 239, 282

Parish, 26, 139, 154, 232, 234, 236, 237, 238, 240, 241
Political parties, 22, 45, 126, 131, 153, 158, 159, 160, 163, 164, 165, 167, 168, 176, 260
Portuguese Constitutionalism, 24, 261, 280
Prime Minister, 23, 116, 120, 172, 182, 183, 185, 186, 200
Principle of constitutionality, 11, 34, 35, 36, 82

Referendum, 20, 22, 23, 45, 96, 127, 139, 142, 143, 144, 145, 146, 147, 148, 149, 150, 151, 152, 153, 154, 166, 173, 184, 197, 232, 260, 264
Religion, 279, 280, 281, 282, 283, 284, 285, 286, 287, 288, 289, 290
Roman Catholicism, 5, 280

Semi-presidential system, 21, 23, 169, 218, 241
Separation of powers, 95, 172
Sovereignty, 10, 11, 12, 13, 16, 17, 33, 51, 124, 127, 173, 204, 205
State of siege and emergency, 68, 261, 262, 264, 267, 268
State of war, 173, 178, 191, 194, 261, 262
Suffrage, 22, 25, 126, 130, 134, 137, 138, 139, 140, 141, 143, 170, 176, 215

Treaties, 20, 87, 90, 91, 143, 153, 173, 180, 184, 185

Written Constitution, 30, 47, 56, 60, 61, 63, 64

Made in the USA
Monee, IL
13 September 2026

62974274R00085